Integrity
Works

Integrity Works

Strategies for
Becoming a
Trusted,
Respected and
Admired Leader

Dana Telford and
Adrian Gostick

With a Foreword by J.W. Marriott III

Gibbs Smith, Publisher
Salt Lake City

First Edition
09 08 07 06 05   10 9 8 7 6 5 4 3 2 1

Published by

Gibbs Smith, Publisher
P.O. Box 667
Layton, Utah 84041
Orders: (1-800) 748-5439
www.gibbs-smith.com

Designed by Gotham Design, NYC
Printed and bound in the United States of America

Library of Congress Cataloging-in-Publication Data
Telford, Dana.
  Integrity works : strategies for becoming a trusted, respected and admired leader /
  Dana Telford and Adrian Gostick.— 1st ed.
        p. cm.
  Includes bibliographical references and index.
  ISBN 1-58685-054-7 (alk. paper)
1. Business ethics—Handbooks, manuals, etc. 2. Corporate
governance—Handbooks, manuals, etc. I. Gostick, Adrian Robert. II. Title.
HF5387.T456 2005
658.4'08—dc22
                                        2004024259

Contents

Acknowledgements 8

Foreword 9

Introduction: Of Mice and Men 12

Chapter 1: You Know That Little Things Count 27
   Integrity Works Case: Hank Greenberg

Chapter 2: You Find the White When Others See Gray 37
   Integrity Works Case: Mary Kay Ash

Chapter 3: You Mess Up, You Fess Up 43
   Integrity Works Case: Mohandas Gandhi

Chapter 4: You Create a Culture of Trust 51
   Integrity Works Case: John Wooden

Chapter 5: You Keep Your Word 59
   Integrity Works Case: Vonetta Flowers

Chapter 6: You Care about the Greater Good 69
   Integrity Works Case: Mother Teresa

Chapter 7: You're Honest but Modest 77
   Integrity Works Case: Katharine Graham

Chapter 8: You Act Like You're Being Watched 85
   Integrity Works Case: Abraham Lincoln

Chapter 9: You Hire Integrity 93
   Integrity Works Case: Warren Buffett

Chapter 10: You Stay the Course 103
   Integrity Works Case: Sir Thomas More

Conclusion: Integrity at Work 113

Sources 121

Acknowledgements

S o many people have been crucial to the development of *Integrity Works*. Thank you Melinda for holding down the fort, for investing your scarce time in reading the manuscript and suggesting ways to make it better. (Abe would thank you if he could!) To Sarah, Alexandra, Rachel, Will and Anna, thanks for sharing Dad's time with others. To Kent and Vicky, thank you for your constant support of my creative ventures and for always believing in me.

Thanks are due to Jennifer and Tony, the light of this author's life, who help him remember what matters most. Thank you also to Joan and Gordon Gostick, and Janet and Robert Raby, wonderful examples of integrity in their own right.

Appreciation is due to Dr. John Davis, whose example of careful thought and hard work continues to be inspirational and amazing. And to Kent Murdock, David Sturt, Chester Elton and other colleagues who exemplify integrity in action.

Thank you to the wonderful leaders quoted herein. To Heather Larson and Christie Giles for your many valuable contributions, research and ideas. To Noah Lapine for providing perspective on an important topic, to Greg Calkins and Tom Morgan for valuable insights at the conceptual stage, and to Don Graham and Ev Small for keeping us on the right track with Katharine.

Much gratitude to Christopher Robbins, Madge Baird, Aimee Stoddard, Alison Einerson, Marty Lee and the rest of the team at Gibbs Smith for helping make book dreams come true.

Foreword

by John W. Marriott III
Executive Vice President, Lodging
Marriott International, Inc.

When asked what qualities we are seeking in future leaders of Marriott, I'm quick to list the characteristics we admire: customer-focused, diligent, intelligent, caring, and the list goes on. But, here's the reality: a person must have integrity. If they don't, they won't last long in our organization.

Integrity is the most important attribute a successful associate, manager or executive can possess. And yet, it seems that people with a strong set of principles are among the hardest to find. When we do find people with integrity, we keep them, we promote them and we ask them to lead others.

In other words, integrity works.

After watching my father, grandfather and many other great Marriott leaders at work, it is obvious that charting a course of integrity each day is critical. Decisions are not always cut-and-dry; however, there are a few simple truths about individuals who possess a great deal of integrity. They are self-aware, they have established their principles and they have determined how they will act prior to any difficult situation. They are consistently open and honest, whether it benefits them or not.

Unfortunately, in business, honesty is not always appreciated. In many organizations, bending "the rules" is too often overlooked. However, a lack of integrity will eventually bring about one's own demise, and an unethical culture will eventually destroy an organization. I believe that organizations with integrity, as described by authors Telford and Gostick, will succeed in the long term.

At Marriott, our success over the past 77 years has been based on hiring good people: caring, dependable associates who are ethical, trustworthy and have a "spirit to serve." Although our company has grown and changed considerably from its humble beginning as a nine-seat root beer stand to a global lodging company with more than 2,600 properties in 64 countries and nearly 130,000 employees, we have never strayed from the basic principles that have made us successful.

We promote people with integrity because we trust them to always do the right thing and to disclose fully when things go wrong. They always provide honest, straightforward direction, and we know we will always be proud of them. People with integrity inspire others and change lives, not usually in dramatic ways, but with quiet, unassuming honesty and trustworthiness. They lead by example.

Businesses and society in general need principled leaders, and I hope you read *Integrity Works* with the aim of improving yourself. This is not just a simple book with a simple message, but the beginning of an important journey to becoming a leader that others will trust, admire and follow. I wish you much success in becoming a true leader.

—John W. Marriott III

Would the boy be proud of the man you are?

— Laurence Peter

INTRODUCTION

OF MICE AND MEN

To Kent Murdock's employees, the idea sounded like career suicide. Murdock had approached them with what he thought was a great idea for a presentation to the management team of his 2,000-employee firm, O. C. Tanner. But when they heard what it was, his executives were stunned into silence.

"You want me to do what?" asked one fellow, finally. "Dress in mouse ears?"

The idea was simple: four members of the leadership team would act out the popular management book *Who Moved My Cheese* to introduce a discussion on change management. O. C. Tanner, an employee-recognition company, was going through more than its share of change—a painful computer system overhaul, an evolution to lean manufacturing and even a transition from pure production to more of a consulting-based services company.

And amid all this stress, heartache and tension, Murdock wanted four executives to dress up like theme park characters—two like mice and two as strange little humanoids who had to adjust to their cheese being moved!

To their credit, Murdock's people didn't immediately reject his idea. Sure, they chuckled a little and shook their heads, but after getting over the initial shock, one by one, they agreed to participate.

Why? Because they trusted their leader.

By the time of the presentation, they were confident of Murdock's plan. In fact, it wasn't Murdock's plan anymore. Each employee had embraced it. It had become their plan.

And you know what? It worked!

"The *Cheese* presentation was a great success," says Murdock. "People still talk about it. It was lighthearted and fun—and a good lead-in to very serious topics for our company.

"Back then, I thought the real success was the presentation itself. Now I realize the true miracle was my employees' trust in me. I now feel greatly honored that they were willing to follow me into the white-collar equivalent of a minefield. And I'm relieved that we all came out of it with our dignity and professionalism intact."

Let's face it, most leaders don't enjoy that kind of relationship with their employees. But Murdock, a winner of the American Business Ethics Award, does. We know because we witnessed the meeting firsthand.

It wasn't long after that skit that we started work on *The Integrity Advantage*, our first book on the subjects of trust, integrity and leadership.

Trust, we realized after much study and experience, is the basis for all successful relationships—in business and in life. And integrity is what inspires trust. It just makes sense, then, that a person who wants to be trusted, followed and admired must first pursue integrity.

And that's the sticky part.

Integrity is a tough taskmaster. It's an action word. It requires constant diligence. In fact, the ability to consistently act in accordance with their own principles is one thing that sets people of integrity apart.

But there are others.

Over the years, we've asked thousands of people to describe the individuals they trust most. Their answers paint a vivid picture:

"Who do I trust? First person who comes to mind is my dad. Is that okay? It doesn't have to be a businessperson, right?"

"No, that's fine. Why your dad?"

"I never saw him tell a lie. And I never saw him exaggerate. That had a big

impact on me. I've been around people who really touted themselves as honest and ethical. And, without exception, it seemed they were trying to convince themselves as much as they were trying to convince others."

"My first supervisor was great . . . really great."

"Why?"

"It was clear she wasn't in it for herself. She would let me meet with the VP all the time, pitching stuff. She never worried about getting credit. She was an amazing team builder. I stayed on her team for years—probably way past the time I could have gotten a better-paying job. But I just couldn't let her down."

"Monsignor LeClaire."

"Your priest?"

"No. He was my department director at a Catholic school where I worked. He was a true servant of his employees."

"A servant? Conventional wisdom says bosses are supposed to be in charge."

"I think the best bosses don't care who is in charge. They want to be, well . . . loved."

"Loved? Really?"

"Yeah. Don't you work harder for people you love? Here's what I mean. When we got our first computers in the department, Monsignor LeClaire delivered them by hand. And that was no small thing. They were the size of Volkswagen Beetles. But he wheeled each one in and helped set them up—scrambling under the desks in his cassock and getting dirty. Not many managers serve you like that."

Though the faces change, people inevitably describe the same key characteristics in people they trust. These answers—and those of leaders like Jim Burke, former CEO of Johnson & Johnson; Shelly Lazarus, chairman and

CEO of Ogilvy Mather Worldwide; and Henry M. "Hank" Paulson Jr., chairman and CEO of Goldman Sachs Group, Inc.—helped us identify the ten universal characteristics exhibited by leaders with integrity. Each of these characteristics is the subject of a chapter of this book:

1. You Know That Little Things Count
2. You Find the White When Others See Gray
3. You Mess Up, You Fess Up
4. You Create a Culture of Trust
5. You Keep Your Word
6. You Care about the Greater Good
7. You're Honest but Modest
8. You Act Like You're Being Watched
9. You Hire Integrity
10. You Stay the Course

Of course, one could argue for additions to the list. Aristotle, for example, might suggest we add courage or gentleness. (And who could argue with Aristotle?) But after years of studying the subject, our research continues to buttress the findings that these ten characteristics form the foundation of leading with integrity.

All of this research, of course, is purely academic . . . until you apply it. The real question, the only question, is how do you match up to the list? To put it even more simply: *do people trust you?*

Even though it sounds like a simple question, it prompts serious introspection:

Sure people trust me . . . well, maybe. I hope. I don't know. Let me think about it. Do my bosses trust me? Do my employees, my clients, my colleagues? Do my kids? I'm pretty sure my family trusts me. But how many people in this world really do trust me? And how deep is their trust? I guess I'm not sure.

If you're like most people, you've never really asked yourself this question. It may never have occurred to you—or you may have avoided the question altogether. And yet, the answer will do more to determine your success in business (and in life) than any other factor. Why?

Because besides possessing similar characteristics, people of integrity share another trait: others are drawn to them. We treasure our relationships with them. A quote by George MacDonald comes to mind: "Few delights can equal the mere presence of one we trust utterly."

For a moment, imagine how your life would change if your employees, colleagues, spouse, children and neighbors treasured their relationships with you.

It can happen. As long as you are willing to become that person.

"Trust" Us: It's Complicated

Contrary to popular belief, there's nothing simple about trust. It's complicated. Or, at least, the kind of trust that this book describes.

On one level, society requires us to trust people simply because of their role or position. For example, we implicitly trust doctors, airline pilots, plumbers, electronics salespeople and even the kids operating the roller coaster ride at the amusement park.

"Keep your hands and arms in the ride at all times. Just two people per seat. No smoking," he barks. (You can almost hear the wind whistling through his tongue ring, can't you?)

We call this kind of trust Capability-Based Trust. It means, "I trust your ability to solve a certain problem or help me at a certain point in time." It's generally short-term and situational. It's founded on perceived aptitude and abilities. We grant it based on subconscious and conscious judgments about a person's credibility. Does this person's age, background, speech, expertise, title, profession, accomplishments and so forth convince me that he or she can successfully solve my problem?

In contrast, trust that is long-term is based on something much harder to define—and earn. We call it Character-Based Trust. This type of trust can only be created over time by consistent behavior, adherence to principles, honesty and dependability. It grows as we watch how a person acts in public and in private. It deepens as we judge someone's motives to be pure and nonthreatening. It leads to loyalty.

Have you ever wondered what could possibly motivate a soldier to follow his sergeant into battle? It's this character-based trust—deep and unwavering. And what allows employees to give their whole hearts and minds to a certain inspiring supervisor? You've got it. It's this same type of trust. (Character-based trust is also what makes a person fall in love with his or her spouse.) Character-based trust is a very powerful, binding emotional tie that all exceptional leaders must create.

Here's how it works. To be a great leader, you must be effective. To be effective, you must be credible. To be credible, you must have integrity built on character-based trust.

And that is where this book comes in.

Writing the Book on Integrity

Whom do you trust? Are you trustworthy? These two simple questions are more important than you may have ever thought. With this book, you will begin to answer them.

That's because the focus of this book is different. It is not just about people facing difficult ethical issues, although we'll stare down a few dilemmas along the way. It's not even about the link between integrity in business and financial success, though we'll give you some compelling evidence of that fact, too. Instead, *Integrity Works* is designed to provide strategies for leaders who are serious about being trusted, followed and admired—whether you want to be a successful Fortune 500 executive, a thriving small-business owner or a better person.

Integrity Works is the sequel to *The Integrity Advantage*, which we were thrilled to watch become a national bestseller after its launch in early 2003. Now, while we'd like to think our research and prose were so compelling that the books flew off the shelf on their own merit, timing was on our side. We began writing the book before Enron and Global Crossing, before Martha Stewart and Arthur Andersen were garnering negative headlines. The book was launched as global brands were being knocked to their knees by public outrage over unethical leadership. The topic was hot and businesspeople wanted answers.

In truth, as we were writing and researching *The Integrity Advantage*, we had little foreshadowing of the dark clouds that would soon gather over the business world. Simply, we had a theory that the most successful leaders and companies over long periods of time have higher levels of integrity than their competitors. Our hypothesis was that impeccable, sustained personal and corporate integrity is a competitive advantage in business.

We had noted with interest work published in *The Business and Society Report* showing that companies that have an effective ethical culture outperformed those that do not by 200 to 300 percent as measured by market value. The report wasn't alone in its findings. Year 2000 research from the Hudson Institute showed that workers in an ethical culture were six times more likely to be loyal than those in unethical cultures, and we're all aware of the multitudinous benefits of loyal employees. Yet another study by *The Conference Board Report* showed 40 percent of consumers were willing to boycott an unethical company, and 25 percent had already done so.

The numbers speak for themselves. Yet, based on these reports and other compelling research, we found at the time that the subject of integrity seemed to be little more than a passing thought at business schools and around corporate boardrooms. Diogenes of Sinope must have been a business major when he wrote, "Discourse on virtue and they pass by in droves; whistle and dance the shimmy, and you've got an audience."

Fortunately, that all was about to change. By the time *The Integrity Advantage* was published, people were speaking of corporate ethics in grocery checkout lines and at soccer games. In fact, today we are pleased to see that integrity is one of the most talked-about issues in the business world. Even more encouraging, we find that many business leaders are implementing the principles of integrity to build organizations with ethical cultures.

In a superb speech a few years ago at Harvard, Norman Lear illustrated the need to return to integrity in business. He said, "Walter Lippman once spoke of the institutions of the church, the family, education and civil authority as 'that old ancestral order,' which was largely responsible for purveying values to society. As those institutions have waned, it is my belief that, inadvertently, American business has come to fill the vacuum. It is now the fountainhead of values in our society."

Lear went on to quote Joseph Campbell: "'In medieval times . . . as one approached a city, the tallest structure on the skyline was the church and its steeple. Subsequently, as the power and influence of the church gave way to kings and rulers, the castle dominated the skyline. Today, as one approaches a city, the most commanding structures are the skyscrapers, the cathedrals of modern business.'

"Today, people are looking to business as the fountainhead of values in our society."

Then Lear paused and asked the provocative question, "Are we delivering?"

Hospira: The Beginnings of Trust
Hospira is one company that is, indeed, delivering. Created in early 2004 as a spin-off of Abbott Laboratories, Hospira was founded with 14,000 employees spread throughout its corporate headquarters, fifteen plants and a handful of distribution centers—from Chicago to Costa Rica to North Carolina to Ireland. It is a $2.5 billion hospital-products company created with four core values, and paramount among those is integrity.

Now, many companies list integrity as a core value. But Chris Begley, CEO of the new company, went a step further. He realized that for employees to make clear decisions, they needed clear direction. So he prioritized his values this way:

1. Integrity
2. Ownership and Accountability
3. Speed
4. Entrepreneurial Spirit

We were fortunate to be invited to speak at the first gathering of the new company leadership, 300 or so strong. At that time, still about four months prior to launch, the organization didn't even have a name. Abbott had given the fledgling outfit several strong product lines and some wonderful leaders—but the values that would guide this independent company would not be solely inherited from Abbott; they would be born at Hospira. Any promises made, any goals established, any culture created, would be introduced by this small, determined group of leaders and their soon-to-be CEO.

Uncertainty was rampant. There were more than a few white knuckles in the audience that December day in Chicago. But one thing was clear within minutes of our arrival: everyone in the room trusted Chris Begley.

Begley is a tall, lanky fellow in his early fifties. He grew up in Chicago, rooting for the White Sox. Over the years with Abbott, he'd steadily risen up the corporate ladder. But was he ready for this challenge? After all, Begley was not a typical Fortune 500 executive. Humility oozes from every pore of his body. He would probably look more at home coaching a Little League team than running a new company bumping up against the ranks of the Fortune 500. But there he was, calm as could be and without a note card in hand, about to address the anxious group.

Thus, in the downtown ballroom, Begley stepped to the microphone and began his remarks. True to form, he started with a non-business approach that captivated his audience:

"When I think of us as an organization," he said, "I inevitably picture a scene from an Indiana Jones movie." Everyone giggled a little, and the mood lightened considerably.

Begley looked around the group. "In it, Indy peers over a thousand-foot crevasse. He has been told there is a bridge; unfortunately, it's invisible. Finally, the resourceful archaeologist reaches down, snatches up a handful of gravel and tosses it over the edge of the cliff. The dirt reveals the bridge is there, after all: a small and uncertain path that remains almost invisible against the backdrop of rock. Still not entirely confident—but understanding there is no turning back—Indy takes his first step. Then another. Trusting. Hoping. Believing.

"At this new company, we are poised at a similar point. We are about to undertake an exciting journey of our own, with a potential for growth previously untapped. Understandably, many of us have our share of butterflies as we take this first giant step toward our future. We must also possess a certain level of trust. Trust in ourselves to fulfill—and exceed—our job responsibilities. Trust in our leadership team to guide this company into growth, new opportunities and prosperity. Trust in team members and managers to live the values of the company, to be honest, forward-looking, and serve the needs of our customers and patients."

Begley paused and looked around the room with a piercing gaze. "That type of trust can only exist in a climate of integrity."

He went on to recount that after the spin-off was announced, he had spent as much time as possible on the road, speaking with future Hospira employees about what he knew about the new company—even though at the time, many details were still unknown.

"The only thing I felt truly confident about was our ability to build an exciting, new global company founded on integrity, so that's what I discussed. And even now with our four core values firmly established, I still place the greatest emphasis on integrity—without reserve."

Begley talked about how important it was that everyone make the right decisions—particularly when confronted with an issue in the "gray area." He recognized that speed is one of the company values, but wisely said it would not be at the expense of integrity or accuracy.

"Search out as many facts as you can discover," instructed Begley, "then ask yourself: 'What is the right answer for all stakeholders?' At this point, you will be prepared to make an educated decision. I also encourage you to seek out people of integrity. Counsel with these mentors concerning difficult situations and follow their lead."

We had suggested to Begley that he cite a specific example of integrity in action during his address. We were honored that he took our advice.

"In particular, I am reminded of one manager's example of integrity," the new CEO added. "He had submitted his impact goals, knowing that the amount of his bonus depended on meeting certain criteria. When he received his bonus, he was surprised. He ran the calculations and said, 'You know, you paid me too much. You need to correct it.' We took a look and, sure enough, he was right. We corrected the mistake and offered a sincere thank-you to this person. To this day, I hold him in the highest regard." (In fact, this manager is now one of Begley's vice presidents.)

Begley kept the audience captivated for twenty minutes, outlining with forthright honesty what he knew and what he didn't know about their future. Finally, he reminded everyone that unless they embraced integrity as a key value, they had nothing at all. "But if each of us practices integrity in dealing with our customers, government agencies, fellow employees and potential new hires, we ultimately will succeed."

He closed by saying, "Picture us achieving our highest expectations. Picture us on top of our industry. Now picture integrity as the bridge that will carry us across the great unknown to the pinnacle of success."

As Begley stepped down from the podium, it was abundantly clear to everyone in the room that the words *integrity* and *buzzword* would never be used in the same sentence at Hospira. Integrity would be the value at the heart of everything this new company would do, and it would define every-thing it would become. Thunderous applause filled the room, and a line of Begley's future Hospira colleagues reached out to shake his hand and pledge their support.

But, of course, the work was just beginning for Hospira. "Since then, I've spent many hours (and sleepless nights) mulling over how best to commu-nicate the vision of integrity within this organization," Begley explained. "It has been the focus of many, many meetings."

Slowly, but with every ounce of effort from people like Stacey Eisen, his vice president of public affairs; Henry Weishaar, his vice president of human resources; and others on his executive and employee team, Hospira is slowly and surely moving along a continuum with one goal: to lead employees on a path from awareness, to understanding, to a deep emotional and personal commitment to their four key values.

And the results? As *Integrity Works* went to press, the new company's first earnings statement surpassed Wall Street's expectations. And, more impor-tantly, as we talk with Hospira employees throughout the organization, they are exceedingly confident about the future. They feel they are valued and empowered. They were completely dedicated to this new company because they know—with a surety—that the company is built on bedrock principles. And foremost among them is integrity.

Faux Integrity
You can get faux anything today, from implants to leather. Some firms are even attempting to imitate a commitment to integrity.

With positive examples like Hospira—and horror stories like Enron—integrity has become the "in" thing in corporate America. Not surprisingly, outplacement firm Challenger Gray & Christmas estimates that one of the three hottest jobs in North America over the next few years will be an ethics executive.

That's good, right? Not always. Ironically, as more companies are realizing the importance of compliance, ethics and integrity in their business dealings—and are filling roles at the very top of the executive chain to make this happen—the gap in execution at the individual level is becoming wider.

One computer programmer we met said, "I just wish you would tell all the executives that read your book that it's not enough to put the word *integrity* in the mission statement if your managers aren't living it. There's a huge gap between what companies say and what managers do. And employees see it."

The programmer we met is right. It is perhaps naive to think that most companies are really becoming more ethical because they appear to be paying closer attention to the issue of ethics, have written standards of conduct and employ an ethics officer.

In the first century A.D., the Roman poet Juvenal asked, "*Sed quis custodiet ipsos custodies?*" Translated, this asks, "But who will watch the watchmen?" The answer today is the same as it was then: we must all be watching—every employee, every manager, every leader, every day. Because as much as the focus of the corporate world may be turning toward integrity as a core principle, only the companies with a true culture of integrity are safe—from themselves.

The following statistic illustrates the problem: just over half the respondents to a 2003 study by the Society for Human Resources Management said they felt pressure to compromise their organization's ethical standards. That's up from just under half of respondents when a similar survey was conducted in 1997. And who do they feel this pressure is coming from? Their leaders.

Do employees want ethical leaders? You bet. According to a study by Steelcase, 85 percent of employees list honesty and ethical dealings as the most-admired virtues of their leaders. Yet only 40 percent of us believe our leaders are actually honest and ethical. That's a performance gap you could drive a Mack truck through.

The result? While many companies try to emulate Hospira's positive example, too many fail because employees still don't trust their leaders. And what happens when employees don't trust the bosses? They feel no commitment to put forth their best effort. Production sags. That puts leaders in a bind, so they look for new ways to hide the downturn from shareholders. And new fuel is thrown on the cycle of deceit.

Why would executives want to sabotage their own companies this way? They don't. They just haven't made the connection between their character and the bottom line. And since our most important work relationship is with our direct supervisor, his or her integrity heavily defines how we feel on the job, how committed we are and how much effort we put forth.

It reminds us of the verse young children recite by Henry Wadsworth Longfellow:

> *And when she was good,*
> *She was very, very good*
> *But when she was bad she was horrid.*

Faux integrity (like most poor imitations) can be an awful thing. But when a company does make the connection between integrity as a corporate value and execution by individual leaders, the results are very, very good. Because, when it comes to integrity, there's nothing like the real thing.

> *I'd rather see a sermon*
> *than hear one any day:*
> *I'd rather one would walk with me*
> *than merely tell the way.*
> —Edgar A. Guest

Getting Integrity to Work for You

Integrity is an action word. Like David Star wrote in *The Philosophy of Danger*, "Wisdom is knowing what to do next; virtue is doing it."

So instead of theory and statistics, this book tells the story of ten individuals who put integrity into action—at all costs. Some have won great rewards. Some haven't. Some are famous. Others you may never have heard of. But each of them illustrates the key characteristics of integrity. And each has left a compelling legacy in his or her wake.

Through their examples, we can learn:

- How to make difficult decisions with integrity
- How to identify integrity in others (i.e., employees, customers, partners, service providers and so on)
- How to build organizations with integrity

And, hopefully, along the way, we can puzzle out a way to live a life of integrity.

So let's start. We'll begin in two unlikely places: a baseball field and a synagogue in Detroit.

Chapter 1

You Know That
Little Things Count

HANK GREENBERG

Integrity Characteristic #1 . . . You Know That Little Things Count

"The only time I ever felt like a hero was on Yom Kippur in Detroit
in 1934 when I walked into the Shaarey Zedek Synagogue unexpected,"
remembered baseball star Hank Greenberg. "The whole audience stood and
applauded while the poor rabbi looked befuddled.
He wasn't sure what had happened."

This is a peculiar statement from a baseball legend who led the American
League in home runs and RBIs in 1935. Why in the world would a batter
who hit fifty-eight home runs in 1938—missing Babe Ruth's record by just
two—say something like that? Read on.

"Hammerin' Hank," as he was affectionately known, played professional
baseball for the Detroit Tigers from 1930 to 1946. Greenberg loved
baseball and played it well. In 1938 (the year he challenged Babe Ruth's
record), he earned the reputation as one of baseball's most feared batters.

But Greenberg was more than that. He was also a leader in the Jewish
community. Not as a rabbi or cantor, but as a role model. Back then, more

than now, athletes accepted the title of role model. Some even saw their fame as an opportunity, a gift that allowed them to try to make the world a better place in their own way. Greenberg was that kind of a player.

His friend Louis Blumberg said, "In those years, there was a little crippled kid who sold pencils outside the ballpark. Worst case of paralysis I ever saw. . . . Hank was always doing things for that kid. He'd have him up for dinner in his suite or the dining room. It was as if he saw something in him . . . that might have been if he hadn't had such a bad break in life."

Greenberg was revered by just about every Jewish kid in Detroit and beyond. Heck, who are we kidding? The adults loved him, too. Tall, powerful and handsome, he was a spectacle whether he stood in the synagogue or at first base. Through his success as a ballplayer, he helped Jews around the country gain acceptance in their mostly non-Jewish communities in a nation that had not yet fully accepted them.

Late in the summer of 1934, the Tigers were battling for the American League pennant. Led by Greenberg's .339 batting average, the Tigers had scratched and clawed from fifth place to first—taking a four-game lead over the powerhouse Yankees.

The stakes were high as the Tigers prepared to begin a series with Boston. It was scheduled to begin on September 10, which, as luck would have it, was also Rosh Hashanah. And that was a problem.

Commonly known as the Jewish New Year's Day, Rosh Hashanah is the first of the Jewish High Holy Days. The second holy day, Yom Kippur—the most important of the Jewish holidays—fell on September 20.

Fans and rabbis nationwide debated whether it was right for Greenberg to play on the High Holy Days. Should he follow his commitment to his faith and people, or should he honor his pledge to his teammates down the last stretch before the playoffs? Dinner tables around the nation buzzed with animated discussion about what Hank Greenberg should and would do.

To understand Greenberg's decision, you've got to know a little about him.

He was born to an orthodox Jewish household January 1, 1911, to David and Sarah Greenberg. He went to high school in the Bronx. He used his strength, height (he stood 6'3" as a teenager) and determination to earn all-city recognition in basketball, soccer and baseball.

But baseball was Greenberg's favorite, and he pursued a career as a ballplayer with true grit and determination. Initially his parents were disappointed in his choice of occupation. A *Detroit Jewish Chronicle* reporter quoted him in 1935 saying, "Jewish women on my block . . . would point me out as a good-for-nothing, a loafer and a bum who always wanted to play baseball rather than go to school. I was Mrs. Greenberg's disgrace."

Greenberg joined the Detroit Tigers organization at age nineteen and spent three years in the minors, playing for Beaumont in the Texas League. Some of Greenberg's teammates had never seen a Jew before. One of them even told Greenberg that he had been told that all Jews had horns.

Greenberg's work ethic was legendary among players. Fearing that his lumbering frame (he was now 6'4" and 215 pounds) hindered rather than helped him, Greenberg worked harder than his teammates. Batting practice was a marathon for him. He often swung his large wooden bat until his hands were torn and bleeding. He earned a championship and MVP honors in the Texas League and joined the Detroit Tigers as a major leaguer in 1933.

He played first base and hit .301 and drove in eighty-seven runs as a rookie. He gained notoriety with fans and fellow players for swinging so hard that his body spun around like a top when he missed. But when he connected, as he often did, the ball sprang from the bat like a bullet from a rifle, and didn't usually return to earth for quite some time.

Greenberg's success in baseball was not rolled out on a red carpet, however. Pre–World War II America was no stranger to anti-Semitism and bigotry. And Detroit was a hotbed for it.

It wasn't surprising, then, that Greenberg caught more than his fair share of verbal heat at the ballpark. "It was a constant thing," Greenberg said in a 1984 interview. "But I used it as a spur to make me do better." Ethnic slurs from fans and opposing players were standard fare. The legendary Dizzie Dean twice called him Mo (short for Moses) while he took batting practice. The New York Yankees went so far as to bring up some notoriously mean minor leaguers who, during a series with the Tigers, were ordered to razz Greenberg.

Most Jewish ball players prior to Greenberg had changed their names to hide their ethnic and religious background. Greenberg wore his Jewish heritage on his sleeve. He never denied it, and he certainly was not ashamed of it. Later in his career, he often said that every home run he had hit was a home run against Adolf Hitler, who at that same time was shoving his message of hatred down Europe's throat.

It's important to note here that Greenberg did not strictly follow the orthodox teachings he was taught as a boy. He leaned more toward Abraham Lincoln's approach to religion: "When I do good, I feel good; and when I do bad, I feel bad." But Greenberg did observe the traditions of his faith out of respect for his heritage, his family and the Jews who admired him.

So here Greenberg was in September of 1934. He had spent the better half of the past two years toiling shoulder to shoulder with his teammates. Their goal was to win the American League pennant and then the World Series. The Tigers enjoyed a fragile lead over the second-place, ever-lurking Yankees. Greenberg was, in his own words, "the only Tiger not in a slump." He was without question their leader, and they looked to him to carry them on the journey to the World Series, to their promised land.

On the other hand, Jewish Americans had gained more acceptance among non-Jews as a result of Greenberg's prowess on the baseball diamond. The Jewish community revered him. He was a source of tremendous pride and unity for them. And, because of that, many wanted him to forgo the games on Rosh Hashanah and Yom Kippur and attend synagogue as a symbol of his commitment to his faith and to his people.

Greenberg thought the matter over and realized this was important to both sides—his fellow players and the Jewish community. So, he came up with his own compromise to satisfy the demands of his clashing principles. He decided he would play on Rosh Hashanah and would attend synagogue on Yom Kippur.

As it turned out, his two solo home runs in that game on Rosh Hashanah single-handedly beat the Red Sox, 2 to 1. He hit the second one in the tenth inning to finish the game. As a show of gratitude the *Detroit Free Press News* ran the headline "Happy New Year!" in Yiddish the day after.

On Yom Kippur, Greenberg skipped the game and attended synagogue, where he was met with a standing ovation. Though the Tigers lost that day, Greenberg's decision moved Edgar A. Guest to write a poem in his honor:

> *Come Yom Kippur—holy fast day wide-world over to the Jew—*
> *And Hank Greenberg to his teaching and the old tradition true*
> *Spent the day among his people and he didn't come to play*
> *Said Murphy to Mulrooney, 'We shall lose the game today!'*
> *We shall miss him in the infield and shall miss him at the bat,*
> *But he's true to his religion—and I honor him for that!*

The Tigers won the American League pennant but lost the World Series to the Cardinals in seven games. A year later, in 1935, the Tigers won the World Series, and Greenberg was the first Jew voted Most Valuable Player in the major leagues.

———————

Greenberg was drafted into the Army in May of 1940. He hit two home runs in his last prewar game and said afterwards, "It's tough to leave baseball, but when your country calls, there's nothing to do but respond."

He took a pay cut of more than 99 percent. His monthly income dropped from $11,000 to $21. Shortly thereafter he was granted an honorable discharge when Congress decided that men over twenty-eight years of age need not serve in the military.

December 1941, however, brought Japanese bombs into Pearl Harbor and thrust the United States into World War II. Again, Greenberg responded courageously. He was the very first major leaguer to enlist, even though he didn't have to. When the Army offered him a safe stateside position as an athletic instructor, Greenberg refused. Instead, he chose to serve in the Army Air Corps in the China-Burma-India theater. He finished his duties there with a distinguished record and returned to America and the Detroit Tigers in the midsummer of 1945.

It didn't take long for him to make himself feel at home again with American League pitching. In dramatic fashion, he hit a home run in his first game back. His success continued. On the last day of the season, he personally clinched the American League pennant for the Tigers by belting a grand slam into the left-field stands. Detroit went on to win the World Series in seven games over the Chicago Cubs. Greenberg played two more seasons and then retired.

Greenberg's career statistics, though shortened by his volunteer military service, are impressive, and leave one wondering, "What if . . . ?" He ended his career with 331 career home runs and 1,276 runs scored. He still holds a number of Detroit Tigers' records, including most doubles in a season (63 in 1934); most home runs in a season (58 in 1938); most RBIs in a season (183 in 1937) and most total bases in a season (397 in 1937).

He played on two World Series championship teams and four All-Star teams. He was named American League Most Valuable Player in 1935 and 1940, and he was the first Jewish player to be inducted into the National Baseball Hall of Fame in Cooperstown, New York, in 1956. He later became a successful team owner and Wall Street investor.

And as for the "what if" questions? What if he had played on Yom Kippur? What if he hadn't volunteered for military service? Well, Greenberg answered that for us long ago:

"When I was playing, I used to resent being singled out as a Jewish ballplayer," he said. "I wanted to be known as a great ballplayer, period. I'm not sure why or when I changed, because I'm still not a particularly religious person. Lately, though, I find myself wanting to be remembered not only as a great ballplayer, but even more as a great Jewish ballplayer."

He got his wish. Henry Benjamin Greenberg died of cancer in Beverly Hills, California, in 1986 at age seventy-five, a great Jewish baseball player, a great person, and a legend on and off the field.

You Know That Little Things Count

Maybe it came from years of focusing on that small, stitched-up cowhide ball: listening for the distinctive "knock" as it sprang from the bat, leaping to snatch it out of midair, the sound of the ball hitting the glove solid in the pocket. Whatever the reason, Hank Greenberg knew that in baseball—and in character—inches count.

He understood that we are much more likely to be judged by the way we handle the hundreds of small decisions we are faced with every day than by the big decisions we make.

After cancer struck Greenberg out in 1986, a *Detroit Free Press* editorial stated, "He gave selflessly to any number of individuals and causes, without issuing self-aggrandizing press releases. Just watch. Praise will flow from places you never considered."

And, boy, did it!

Fan Ben Rose of Southfield, Michigan, recalled, "In 1938 the Tigers had paid for the United Hebrew schools to see a game. In about the seventh inning, Hank came lumbering out to left field as usual and my friend Joe, as a joke, yelled to him in Yiddish that he was hungry. Hank turned around and called over to the peanut vendor and told him to give us each a box of peanuts and charge it to him."

Dr. Harold Bussey of Southfield remembered, "A few years ago, Hank was one of the first to charge for his autograph, but the checks were [to be] made out to Pets Adoption, his favorite charity. Only a few of us knew that Hank matched every dollar sent in out of his own pocket."

And our personal favorite from Harriet (Greenberg) Colman, also of Southfield: "As a young teenager, I had a tremendous crush on Hank Greenberg. The year 1936 was a leap year in which a female could propose marriage to a male. I sent a written proposal of marriage to Hank. He answered my proposal with a friendly handwritten note to the effect that he wasn't quite ready to marry at that time. Of course, I was thrilled to have a personal note from my hero—never dreaming that anything further would develop.

"However, shortly thereafter, I learned that he was to be a guest speaker at the youth group meeting of Congregation Shaarey Zedek. Of course, I attended. I was a very shy thirteen-year-old, but I found the courage to introduce myself to this gorgeous hunk as the girl who had proposed to him. With a number of members of the youth group present, he looked at me and with a twinkle in his eye said, 'I accept.' It was an unforgettable moment when Hank made a starry-eyed teenager feel very special."

Baseball fan Bill O'Neill says Greenberg was part of a rare and dying breed: "You don't see players like him anymore. He was talented, but he was a great model for the kids, too. We used to see him walking up Michigan Avenue to games and he always treated people kindly. That's what kind of guy he was."

Funny, isn't it? Few people mentioned box scores, although they obviously knew of his prowess on the ball field. They didn't recall particular home runs or plays. No, in their minds, what set Hank Greenberg apart was that he was a good person.

It's what sets us apart as leaders, too. In today's world, few things seem to shock people anymore—except integrity. In the play *Blithe Spirit*, Noel Coward wrote, "It's discouraging to think how many people are shocked by honesty and how few by deceit."

Even more unusual are leaders who recognize their responsibility to act with integrity—for the benefit of those around them. Greenberg was one of those people.

His decision to sit out the game on Yom Kippur was made for the benefit of his Jewish fans. Though Greenberg wasn't particularly religious himself, he knew the holiday was important to many of those who looked up to him. He also knew that even a leader's smallest action can ultimately have a very large impact on the character of those who are watching.

A simple example of this principle is a farm gate, the kind that blocks access to a private road. At the hinge, the gate never moves more than a few inches. The movement is hardly noticeable. At the other end, however, it swings far and wide—opening enough to allow large farm equipment and large farm animals to pass through. One small movement at our end may have a huge influence far away.

Greenberg understood all of this. In the Aviva Kempner documentary film *The Life and Times of Hank Greenberg*, he said, "The privilege of being a ballplayer [is] that there is some inspiration to kids that look up to you that makes heroes out of you. I've tried to pattern my life on the fact that I'm out there in the limelight, so to speak, and that there are a lot of kids out there, and if I set a good example for them that maybe it will in some way affect their lives."

Now you might be thinking, "No one looks up to me." But you might be surprised. As leaders of teams, families or corporations, we possess incredible power for good. By the same token, it's amazing how quickly one small step in the wrong direction can put us on a journey we never expected to start.

"He who permits himself to tell a lie once, finds it much easier to do it a second and a third time, till at length it becomes habitual; he tells lies without attending to it, and truths without the world's believing him. This falsehood of the tongue leads to that of the heart, and in time depraves all of its good dispositions," said Thomas Jefferson in a letter to Peter Carr on August 19, 1785.

Frank VanderSloot, president and CEO of Melaleuca, a $600-million consumer products company, explained deception this way: "As a kid, people start out stealing candy bars, not cars. The fraud you see happening in corporations on a large scale started out on a small scale. People justify wrongdoing in their minds: the company owes me this. But then it grows and fraudulent behavior becomes easier to justify. It can start with a pilfered pen or another simple deception. After a few years, you have an employee who is willing to extort thousands of dollars."

That's why at VanderSloot's company, employees are taught to take the high road on everything, especially the seemingly trivial.

"Little things count," he says. "Like when someone calls in to talk to a manager and [his] assistant says [he is] in a meeting when [he is] not. It's the little things that your employees notice. So we teach employees that we never lie. The assistant may say the manager cannot take the call right now, but we do not make up stories. We will not say anything that is untrue."

And that's really it in a nutshell: never say anything that is untrue. And never give a false impression. People of integrity know that little things count; therefore, they never speak or act deceptively. It's absolutely critical if you want to be a trusted, respected and admired leader.

And nowhere is integrity more apparent than in the life of Hank Greenberg. He understood that being a straight hitter (even in the small things) was more important than hitting a home run any day.

And that's one of the most important things any leader—in any field—could ever know.

Chapter 2

You Find the White When Others See Gray

MARY KAY ASH

Integrity Characteristic #2 . . . You Find the White When Others See Gray

It was 1963. Texas. And Mary Kay was fired up. She had just resigned as national sales director for World Gifts after her male assistant had been promoted over her at twice her salary. She had a husband, three grown children and twenty-five years of direct sales experience. But she wasn't ready to retire.

So she decided to start a cosmetics business. Blessed with natural energy and optimism, she knew she was the right person to train, supervise and motivate the beauty consultants who would sell her products. She and her husband agreed that he would tend to the business details such as accounting and finance.

Sometimes only tragedy can clear your vision and slow your pace. Over breakfast, one month prior to the scheduled launch of the new company, Mary Kay and her husband were reviewing the budget for their new venture. Before the meal ended, he was dead, the tragic victim of a major heart attack.

Fast forward to 1980. Despite the death of her first husband, Mary Kay Ash (now married to Mel Ash, whom she wed in 1966) had managed to pick up the pieces and was now at the top of her game. She was the female CEO of a hugely successful, publicly traded company. Her wealth had grown dramatically in a short period of time. Mary Kay Cosmetics, her creation, her dream company, had topped $100 million in sales just one year earlier. Women around the world were buying and selling her pretty, pink-packaged cosmetics. Pink Cadillacs were instantly recognized as the prize of a successful Mary Kay sales consultant. She was a sought-after motivational speaker and one of just a few female CEOs in the country.

Then tragedy struck again. Her beloved Mel, husband of fourteen years, was diagnosed with cancer. His doctors were unsure of its seriousness. They could not say whether or not it was terminal.

Ash was stunned. Not only that, she was confused. You see, one year prior to Mel's diagnosis, the General Federation of Women's Clubs had hired Ash to be the keynote speaker at their annual convention in St. Louis in June 1980. And the date was rapidly approaching.

Thousands of women had registered and paid for the event. Plans had been made, hotel rooms booked, airfare purchased. Mel knew Mary Kay would want to stay by his bedside and break the commitment she had made to the group. He insisted that he would be fine and that she should travel to St. Louis and keep her promise.

To Ash the decision was heart wrenching. She felt a deep sense of responsibility to the man she loved and to her commitment to speak at the convention. She had looked forward to teaching so many women about the Mary Kay philosophy. The advice she had given to others echoed painfully in her torn heart and mind: "Whatever you say, you will do, even if you have to move heaven and earth." On the other hand, she had counseled others to get their priorities in order, and then "press on, and never look back."

She looked to her core principles for help, which were the source of the guiding principles of her company: God first, family second, career third. How often had she quoted this motto in media interviews, in speeches and in company meetings? Now in a time of hardship, the decision was so clear.

She sent one of her top national sales directors, Dalene White, to St. Louis to speak in her place. Mary Kay stayed by Mel's side for the next seven weeks, weeks that ended up being their last together.

It had been the right decision. The grayness, all the confusion, had vanished when she held her decision to stay home with Mel up to her motto. Her motto had never let her down before. And it hadn't this time, either.

You see, from the split second Ash had decided to start her company, she knew it would be different; it would be special. Her idea for making it special was not novel or grandiose. She used her simple motto (God first, family second, career third) and the Golden Rule.

She said, "I chose as my standard the Golden Rule: 'Do unto others as you would have them do unto you.' Some might consider it corny and old-fashioned, but no one can deny its simple truth. Imagine how much better our world would be if everyone lived by this creed."

Armed with a strong product, the support and encouragement of her children, and sound principles, she set out with a clear, rock-solid purpose: to provide women with an unlimited opportunity for personal and financial success. She was determined to lead her company forward with unbending values. She expected a lot of herself, and of the women who represented her company.

She explained, "We need leaders who work for the benefit of others and not just for their own personal gain; who inspire and motivate rather than intimidate and manipulate; and who follow a moral compass that points in the right direction regardless of the trends."

And she succeeded. No other company in history has provided the opportunities Mary Kay has for women in the United States. The story is an entrepreneurial emerald. From its humble beginnings, Mary Kay,

Inc., has grown to become the second largest direct seller of skin-care products in the United States. In 2003, more than 1.3 million independent Mary Kay sales consultants sold $1.8 billion of beauty products in thirty countries. *Fortune* magazine recently recognized the company as one of the "100 Best Companies to Work for in America," and among the ten best companies for women.

Obviously, looking back on her career, it's plain that Ash did a lot of things right. She credits much of that success to following her motto: "My priorities have always been God first, family second, career third. I have found that when I put my life in this order, everything seems to work out."

During her later life, Ash had a habit of closing many of her letters and speeches with the poem "On Silver Wings." She had come upon it during a trip to Australia in 1971 to launch the company's first subsidiary. It spoke to her, so she kept it in her mind and heart. Today, it remains at the core of the Mary Kay culture. It goes like this:

> *I have a premonition that soars on silver wings.*
> *It is a dream of your accomplishment,*
> *Of many wondrous things.*
> *I do not know beneath which sky,*
> *Or where you'll challenge fate.*
> *I only know it will be high,*
> *I only know it will be great.*

Ash knew something about challenging fate—about how gray it can seem at times at the heights of leadership. She also understood the promise of greatness. At the core, she knew that integrity ensured success.

You Find the White When Others See Gray

Ash isn't the only one with a theory on how to succeed in business and life. In the marvelous children's book *Harry Potter and the Sorcerer's Stone*, the character Professor Quirrell explains his approach to life. Not surprisingly, it is the polar opposite of the cosmetic giant.

Quirrell (like most of us) exited school with a pretty clear-cut understanding of good and evil. Then he met Lord Voldemort. "Lord Voldemort showed me how wrong I was," said Quirrell. "There is no good and evil, there is only power, and those too weak to seek it."

Put in writing, Quirrell's theory sounds obscene. But his theory isn't new. Managers communicate it all the time by encouraging success at all cost. Leaders often look the other way when unscrupulous business practices might lead to profit.

And while we might see right through it most of the time, we're more susceptible to it when we find ourselves in a gray area. It's when we are faced with these "in-between" decisions that we typically need help. Sometimes a boss, parent, coworker, friend, mentor or sibling can help us make difficult decisions. Or it might be a policy, a rule or a law that stands firm when a questionable course of action is thrown against it.

But the very best guide when we are faced with a gray area is our personal priorities. It's what Ash fell back on. In determining a difficult course of action, she held it up against the light of her priorities: God first, family second and company third. When she did this, she found that the right decision became clear and crisp, like a developing picture.

The late Ivy Lee, an efficiency consultant to major corporations, also understood the power of priorities. In the early 1900s, he approached Charles Schwab, then president of Bethlehem Steel Company, with an interesting proposal: "If I could increase your efficiency and sales by spending just fifteen minutes with each of your executives, would you hire me to do the job?"

"How much would it cost?" asked Schwab.

"Nothing," replied Lee, "unless I'm successful. Take three months to decide and then pay me whatever you feel it is worth."

Schwab agreed to it, and Lee went to work.

As the story goes, three months passed and Schwab sent Lee a check for $35,000 (keep in mind, this was more than seventy-five years ago).

What had Lee told each executive that was worth that type of money?

He just asked them to make a simple promise. For the next ninety days, he asked them to promise to list the six most important things they needed to accomplish the next day, and then prioritize them. When they arrived at work, they were to begin working on those six items, scratch them off when they were completed and move to the next tasks. They were to add uncompleted tasks to the next day's list.

The knowledge that cost Schwab $35,000 you get for the price of this book. In a nutshell, before you can do what is most important, you have to know what is most important.

And that begs the question, "What is most important to you?" Once you know the answer, decision-making is greatly simplified.

On the other hand, if you never take the time to set priorities, it's easy to get off track. You've heard quotes like, "If you don't know where you're going, you're guaranteed to get there." And, "Don't spend your life getting to the top of the ladder, only to find it's leaning against the wrong fence." We hear these so often because they're . . . true.

Priorities help you to know where you are and where you are going at all times. And they give you the ethical backbone to hold your ground when push comes to shove.

"In matters of style, swim with the current; in matters of principle, stand like a rock." Ash loved this quote by Thomas Jefferson. And she lived it. By identifying and prioritizing her principles, and then making up her mind to adhere to them, no matter how dangerously the waters swirled around her, she was able to find the white when others saw gray. Her acute moral vision allowed her to lead others quickly and decisively in the right direction.

As a result, Mary Kay Ash usually found herself "in the pink." And so can we.

Chapter 3

You Mess Up, You Fess Up

MOHANDAS GANDHI

Integrity Characteristic #3 . . . You Mess Up, You Fess Up

Mohandas Gandhi was wavering. Raised in a strict Hindu home in India, he had promised his mother, Putlibai, that he would remain a vegetarian throughout his life. He respected and admired his mother. She was a strong person of character, who attended religious services every day. Living with such an example of self-denial and conscience, Gandhi had never questioned the wisdom of his pledge. But now, things were changing.

At school, Gandhi had heard of a reform movement in his country. His friend, Sheik Mehtab, told him that many of India's greatest leaders— even some of their teachers—were secretly taking meat. Gandhi's older brother was one of them.

"I was surprised and pained," wrote Gandhi. "I asked my friend the reason and he explained it thus: 'We are a weak people because we do not eat meat. The English are able to rule over us because they are meat-eaters. You know how hardy I am, and how great a runner, too. It is because I am a meat-eater. Meat-eaters do not have boils or tumors, and even if they happen to have any, these heal quickly. Our teachers and other distinguished people who eat meat are not fools. They know its virtues. You should do likewise. There is nothing like trying. Try, and see what strength it gives.' "

His friend's persuasive arguments in favor of meat-eating continued for some time. And, slowly, Gandhi began to see meat-eating in a different light. He certainly looked feeble compared with his friend and brother. Weren't they stronger and more daring than he? Couldn't his friend high jump and long jump with skill? The frail Gandhi began to feel a strong desire to be like them. More than that, he began to believe that meat-eating was necessary if the people of India were ever to overthrow English rule.

Every day, the chant of the schoolboys echoed in his head:

> Behold the mighty Englishman,
> He rules the Indian small.
> Because being a meat-eater,
> He is five cubits tall.

"All this had its due effect on me," said Gandhi. "I was beaten. It began to grow on me that meat-eating was good, that it would make me strong and daring, and that, if the whole country took to meat-eating, the English could be overcome."

Convinced that it was his patriotic duty, the boy Gandhi—who would grow to be called Mahatma or "Great Soul"—met his friend at a lonely spot near the river to try his first meat. The dried goat meat was tough and unpleasant. Gandhi became sick after he tasted it.

"I had a very bad night afterwards. A horrible nightmare haunted me. Every time I dropped off to sleep, it would seem as though a live goat were bleating inside me, and I would jump up full of remorse. But then I would remind myself that meat-eating was a duty and so become more cheerful."

The next time Gandhi and Sheik Mehtab met to eat meat, his friend had gone to great lengths to make the meal more palatable. They went to an elegant statehouse. This time, instead of tough goat meat, the friend had arranged for a chef to prepare various delicacies with meat. Gandhi enjoyed about a half dozen such visits before the guilt of deceiving his parents took its toll. For although Gandhi would question many aspects of traditional Hinduism over his lifetime—even the very existence of God—his belief in a moral code rooted in truth only grew stronger and stronger. His deception was torture to his conscience.

"Therefore I said to myself: 'Though it is essential to eat meat, and also essential to take up food reform in the country, yet deceiving and lying to one's father and mother is worse than not eating meat. In their lifetime, therefore, meat-eating must be out of the question.' "

He told his friend this, confessed his transgression to his parents and never consumed meat again. His journey to becoming a truly great soul had begun.

———————

Decades later, Gandhi lay ill and dying. In desperation, his doctors tried to persuade *bapuji*, or "father," to drink a little beef broth. It might very well save his life, they told him. Certainly, in this case, the end would justify the means, they urged. Hadn't they treated many other good Hindus who had not objected to this course of treatment, with good results? After all, it was a little thing. And under the circumstances . . .

But this time Gandhi did not waver. In the years since he had taken meat in his youth, Gandhi had chosen "the path of truth," as he called it. This vow took first place in his life—even above continuing that life. To the doctor, he replied, "There is only one course open to me: to die, but never to break my pledge."

He did not die, but lived to face the same decision—during serious illnesses of his wife and ten-year-old son. He knew that encouraging them to eat meat could help them get better. It was never easy. But, according to his moral code, he was secure in his knowledge that it was not right to eat meat.

"Three things cannot long be hidden: the sun, the moon, and the truth."
— Confucius

You Mess Up, You Fess Up

The more you study the life of Gandhi, the more you understand what a dedicated life he led. He spun 200 yards of thread each day. He wore only handmade cloth. He fasted frequently for political and spiritual reasons. And he gave away most of his earthly possessions. When he was assassinated in 1948, he owned only a few bowls, spoons, a watch, two pairs of sandals and a book of songs.

Of Gandhi, Albert Einstein said, "Generations to come . . . will scarce believe that such a one as this ever in flesh and blood walked upon this earth."

Yet for all his strength of character, you also come to understand that, at times, Gandhi faltered. You've just read about his struggle with meat, which he won. But perhaps the greatest challenge he faced was giving up dairy products, which he never did.

He had been taught that it was wrong, and he believed it was wrong to drink milk. "It is my strong conviction that the human being doesn't need milk, except for the mother's milk he gets as a baby. His diet should consist exclusively of fruits and nuts," he wrote.

Nevertheless, after six years of abstinence, he returned to goat milk, drinking it during his noon and evening meals. This failing pained him greatly. He regretted his weakness. But like his openness about his struggle with eating meat, Gandhi never tried to hide his failings.

"A principle is a principle, and in no case can it be watered down because of our incapacity to live it in practice," he wrote. "We have to strive to achieve it, and the striving should be conscious, deliberate and hard."

He later described his habit of drinking goat milk as "the tragedy of my life."

Another time, one of his correspondents accused him of violating his vow of truth by purposely misreading a letter. (Interestingly enough, Gandhi had supposedly misread it in the writer's favor.) Gandhi replied, "One who follows truth is never guilty of untruth in word or deed even unknowingly. . . . According to this definition, I certainly lapsed from truth. My only consolation is that I never claim anything beyond a sincere endeavor to keep the vow of truth. It never happens that I tell a lie deliberately. I do not remember having deliberately told a lie any time in my life, except on one occasion when I cheated my revered father." (The event he describes with his father occurred when he was a young boy.)

Through his struggles, Gandhi taught a principle that would serve us all well: the real error is not in making a mistake; it is in attempting to cover it up. Failure is an inherent part of the process of innovation. If you are in an environment that won't tolerate occasional honest mistakes, you are probably in a diseased culture.

Regrettably, few leaders understand this.

James E. Burke, CEO of Johnson & Johnson during the Tylenol poisonings, was fortunate to learn it early in his career. As a young product director at J&J, Burke attempted to market over-the-counter medicines for children. It was an unsuccessful venture, and the CEO, General Johnson himself, called him in.

"I assumed I was going to be fired," said Burke in an interview with *Fortune* magazine. "But instead, Johnson told me, 'Business is about making decisions, and you don't make decisions without making mistakes. Don't make that mistake again, but please be sure you make others.' "

It's a lesson Burke put into practice when seven people died in 1982 after ingesting Tylenol capsules poisoned with cyanide. J&J removed Tylenol capsules from the shelves and replaced bottles that consumers had purchased—at a cost of more than $100 million dollars.

But the part of the story that we find most revealing you might not have heard at all. And that's because J&J fessed up immediately.

It was the day after the first deaths were announced. If Burke thought things couldn't get worse—he was wrong. To his horror, he discovered that the statement J&J had made the day before—that no cyanide was kept on company premises—was false. It was the worst possible time to be inaccurate. It would undoubtedly raise suspicion that the tampering had occurred at the manufacturing plant and that some degree of cover-up was taking place. So what did J&J do?

They contacted the media with the correction.

The rest is history. Because of their honesty, what could have been a mountain of negative press for J&J was reduced to a molehill. Some would even argue that it boosted the company's credibility. There certainly is compelling evidence to support that theory.

In 1986, just two weeks after a second rash of cyanide poisonings forced J&J to remove Tylenol capsules permanently from the world market, President Ronald Reagan told Jim Burke, "You have our deepest appreciation for living up to the highest ideal of corporate responsibility and grace under pressure."

So, are we saying that making mistakes (and taking responsibility) will win you the favor of presidents and kings? Not always. But it may save your company (or personal reputation) from a slow and painful death.

Gandhi put it this way: "If ever again you happen to commit a wrong, you should not sleep over your confession. It is human to err. Therefore one is bound to commit an error, but that in itself is not a very grave matter. The danger lies in hiding that error. When a person resorts to untruth to make mistakes one after another, it can be very harmful. If there is an abscess in the body, one can press it and remove the pus. But if the poison is not removed and it spreads in the body it may result in death."

In recent years, we have witnessed the very public demise of some of the most promising organizations in corporate America. The cause: the poison of dishonesty spreading rampantly through the system.

The difficulty is that there are always many compelling reasons to avoid fessing up. We often rationalize:

- People will think badly of me.
- What they don't know won't hurt them.
- If anyone finds out, this could ruin my career.

• It's not really illegal, in a strict sense. It's more of a gray area.

And the biggest excuse of all for covering up wrongdoing (drum roll, please): I didn't have any other choice.

That is the biggest self-deception of all. In a personal letter, Gandhi wrote: "He alone is a lover of truth who follows it in all conditions of life. Nobody is forced to tell lies in business or in service. One should not accept a job which does so, even if one starves in consequence."

It's a nice way of saying that integrity isn't for wimps. And he was absolutely right. The very act of rising to the occasion and taking responsibility for our mistakes opens us up to lose something: money, position, pride, opportunity. By the same token, there is much to be gained, like the respect of those around us. Gandhi put it this way: "People of stainless character will easily inspire confidence and automatically purify the atmosphere around them."

By fessing up, you create an atmosphere of trust. And within an atmosphere of trust, it is much easier for people to achieve and excel. As Burke said, "Nothing good happens without trust. With it, you can overcome all sorts of obstacles. You can build companies that everyone can be proud of."

More that that, you can become a person you can be proud of. And that is a great success indeed.

Chapter 4

You Create
a Culture of Trust

INTEGRITY WORKS CASE

JOHN WOODEN

Integrity Characteristic #4 . . . You Create a Culture of Trust

No one has ever accomplished what John Wooden did. And perhaps no one ever will again.

During the 1950s and '60s, he amassed an unbelievable record as the head men's basketball coach at the University of California, Los Angeles (UCLA): four perfect 30-0 seasons, eighty-eight consecutive victories, thirty-eight straight NCAA tournament victories, twenty PAC-10 championships and ten national championships. Under his guidance, UCLA won seven national championships in a row. He won more than 80 percent of the basketball games he coached. He was NCAA Basketball Coach of the Year six times.

But Wooden's real genius wasn't his ability to win titles. It was his ability to build a culture of trust.

———————

Take the story of a young African-American man who played at Indiana State during Wooden's first year there. The kid was a freshman who didn't get many minutes on the court. But he was part of the team.

The National Association of Intercollegiate Athletics (NAIA) invited

Indiana State to play in their tournament. In 1946, black players were not allowed to play in the NAIA. Wooden rejected the invitation for that reason.

The NAIA called again the following year to invite Indiana State to play in the tournament. Wooden again refused based on the same principle.

But this time this young man's parents and the National Association for the Advancement of Colored People thought there might be value in going. Wooden was persuaded.

During a stopover at a restaurant in Illinois on the way to St. Louis, the young man was refused entrance. Wooden and the rest of the team turned and left, saying, "You take us all or you do not take any." They were happy to eat takeout somewhere else, together.

In St. Louis, the young man wasn't allowed to stay in the hotel, wasn't allowed to eat in the restaurants, but he was part of the team and they sat together during games. According to Wooden, the young man was accepted and there were no problems. Thanks, in part, to Coach Wooden, that young man became the first African-American to take part in the NAIA tournament.

About the incident, Wooden said, "There's way too much prejudice in this world, not just in race, but in religion and other ways. It was just my upbringing that you never looked down on anyone for any reason at all, and certainly not race or religion. Anything anyone can do to help it, even if it's just a little, that's good. We are many, but are we much? We're not much until we all contribute to some degree."

By standing up for his principles, and for members of his team (even the non-starters), Wooden gained the trust of his players, and created a trusting atmosphere. Players knew that he cared about their performance as players as well as their development as people. This allowed them to dedicate themselves wholeheartedly to the advancement of the team.

Ask any of the hundreds of young men who played for him, and they'll say Wooden was the finest basketball coach on the planet, and one of the finest people. Even to this day, decades after playing for him, they respect and trust "Coach" completely. Why? Certainly because he is a competent leader, but more so because the strength of his character shaped theirs. By example, he taught them guiding principles and helped them see the potential that lay dormant inside them. He opened their eyes to what they could become.

Wooden took his coaching responsibility very seriously. In his own words, he called leadership "a sacred trust: helping to mold character, instill productive principles and values, and provide a positive example to those under my supervision." His players have been the beneficiaries of his dedication to his craft.

"He wasn't just teaching us about basketball, he was teaching us about life. He taught us how to focus on one primary objective: be the best you can be in whatever endeavor you undertake," said Bill Walton, NBA Hall of Fame player.

"His wisdom had a profound influence on me as an athlete, but an even greater influence on me as a human being. He is responsible, in part, for the person I am today," said Kareem Abdul-Jabbar, also an NBA Hall of Famer.

Leaders who approach their team this way build trust, strand by strand, like the individual strings that create the strength of a rope. The team as a whole is much stronger and much greater than the sum of the individual strings.

So what can a basketball coach teach business leaders about building a culture of trust? Coach Wooden understood that people must trust and respect their leader before they can truly become an outstanding team. He knew that that meant setting expectations for himself and his players early.

For that reason, Wooden held meetings with players two weeks before their first practice to set expectations for their behavior. He made it clear that they were to be courteous to team managers and pick up after themselves. He explained specifically how they were to look and act: no long hair, no mustaches and no long sideburns.

Despite this, the year after Lew Alcindor (Kareem Abdul-Jabbar) graduated, two promising young players returned to UCLA. They showed up for the team picture with muttonchops that they'd been growing for a few months.

Coach Wooden didn't give them uniforms. When they asked him why, he stated, "I'm not going to explain it again to you. You have fifteen minutes to go see Ducky Drake, our trainer, and let him get busy with his razor and clippers and get you in shape." They turned on their heels and got razored by Ducky.

Coach Wooden believes they were testing him and his commitment to his principles, especially now that the "big guy" Lew Alcindor had graduated. They figured maybe he'd let them get away with a breach because he needed them. Wooden, however, knew they would have lost respect for him had he shifted his stance.

"What would that have done to the rest of my team if I had given in to them?" he mused.

One look at the chaos running rampant in many American corporations says it all.

You Create a Culture of Trust

A lot of managers place trust issues firmly on the "soft side" of business. To them, it's a touchy-feely thing, and something that is "nice to have," but certainly not a "must have." But in reality, trust is a profit maker.

Paul Zak, professor of economics at Claremont University, has researched the economic effects of trust in societies. He has found that trust in a society is highly correlated with economic growth. Trust encourages savings and investment and reduces the transaction costs associated with doing business. Unfortunately, when less than 30 percent of people in a society trust other people, it is likely that poverty will get worse.

Keeping that in mind, the following statistics paint a telling picture. Only 5 percent of people in Peru trust one another. In Norway, the figure is 65 percent. Forty-four percent of United Kingdom citizens trust one another. And in the United States, the figure is 36 percent.

But, wait, there's more. In the United States, three out of four people don't believe there is any correlation between what campaigning politicians promise to do and what they will actually do if elected. Two of three don't trust even long-standing companies to make safe, durable products without the government setting industry standards. And 55 percent believe that companies will take advantage of the public if they think they can get away with it.

There's no way around it. We've got a growing trust problem on our own soil. And it's destined to make us less competitive in global markets; spend too much money on contracts, disputes and litigation; and burden us with inefficiencies. That is, unless we can turn it around. To do so, we need leaders to take the first step.

Some years ago while in graduate school, I (Dana) returned home for the December holidays. As I shopped at my hometown mall, I found myself scanning the passing faces, looking for someone I recognized. My eyes met those of a familiar fellow about my age. I stuck out my hand and smiled and said hello.

He took the proffered hand, smiled, cocked his head to the side and said, "Remind me of your name again."

I said, "I'm Dana. And you are . . . "

"John."

"Right, John. Good to see you. How are things going?"

"Great," he replied. "Work is good. I'm an architect. You?"

"Things are great. I'm in graduate school in Boston. I'm married. Two kids. Any kids for you?" I asked.

"Not yet, one on the way though," John replied.

Our polite chat continued for what was probably another five minutes before John stopped, stood up a bit straighter, took a deep breath and said, "You know, Dana, I'm convinced that we've never met before today."

By that point, I was convinced of the same. I said, "I think you're right. It's been real nice talking with you though. Have a great day."

He said, "You too. Good to meet you," shook my hand and walked away.

That story always makes people laugh. Some of the people I share it with then tell me about a similar occurrence in their life. For years, I've wondered why it happens; and I think I've finally figured it out. It has a lot to do with something called the Norm of Reciprocity.

The Norm of Reciprocity is a part of human nature. It crosses all cultures. It means, in simple terms, that we respond in kind to how we're treated. Kind of like a pre–Golden Rule thing. We do unto others as we're done unto.

To understand it, think, for a moment, what happens when you are approached by someone who is smiling and has their hand out to shake? Chances are overwhelming that any person in any place at any time will smile and grasp the offered hand. Try it on a stranger sometime.

Louis Barnes, professor emeritus at Harvard Business School, uses the Norm of Reciprocity to help people understand how trust affects any relationship. His theory is straightforward and powerful: if one person decides to trust another, the Norm of Reciprocity says he or she will most likely be trusted in return.

This affects behavior. If I trust you and you trust me, then we're on the same team, which means we'll cooperate, work together to solve problems and help each other. And if I help you first, you might even do more for me than I did for you. (This is called Constructive Reciprocity.) All parties involved succeed.

Now let's consider what Professor Barnes calls the World of Mistrust. If we are forced to work together in some capacity (real estate transaction, inter-company task force, etc.) and I decide not to trust you, I will view you with suspicion and skepticism. You are someone to be wary of—a potential enemy.

If I don't trust you—even if I never tell you that fact openly—chances are high that you won't trust me, either. We will begin to behave as enemies. Since you are my enemy, I focus on winning the battle. I must be prepared to fight. I defend myself, attack you and withdraw when it suits my purposes.

You do the same. If I injure you, you seek to not only injure me in return, but also to inflict more damage and hurt. (This is known as Destructive Reciprocity.) In this type of battle, as in most battles, one side wins and one side loses.

Of course, it is foolish to trust everyone all of the time, and just as foolish never to trust anyone. In this regard, we agree with our Middle Eastern client who likes to say, "Trust in Allah, but tie up your camel." The point here is that it pays to begin our relationships trusting and believing in people. If we trust others, chances are we'll be trusted in return. Leaders demonstrate trust by raising their expectations of the people who follow them—and holding firm to clear standards. As they do, employees generally rise to the occasion and fulfill (if not exceed) expectations.

Doug Shannon, who works in client operations at Baltimore-based investment management firm T. Rowe Price, is a great example of this principle. When his manager took an extended maternity leave, he volunteered to do double duty—his job and hers. It was a tough assignment—and in many companies another "leader" would have been asked to move over and help. But enlightened management at T. Rowe Price let Shannon, who had no supervisory experience, take on the assignment.

Shannon stepped up to the challenge—and the team didn't miss a beat. He became even more committed to his company and his work. Why? Because he was trusted.

Simply put, if you treat people at the level they are, there they will stay. If you treat people at the level they can be and should be, they often stretch to that higher level.

––––––––––––––––

At the time this book went to press, John Wooden was nearly ninety years old. On the twenty-first of each month he sits down and writes a love note to the only girl he ever dated, his wife, Nellie. Then he adds it to the stack on her pillow. They are all unopened. Nellie passed away fifteen years ago.

John Wooden created a culture of trust through caring and consistency with Nellie and with his teams. His players trusted his coaching abilities, his vision, his understanding of the game and his character. They knew that whatever Coach asked them to do, no matter how difficult, was for the good of the whole team. And that inspired them to work harder at improving themselves—both on the court and off.

By the way, 180 young men played for him over the years. He still knows where 172 of them are today, twenty-nine years after retiring.

Chapter 5

You Keep
Your Word

VONETTA FLOWERS

Integrity Characteristic #5 . . . You Keep Your Word

When Vonetta Flowers traded her track shoes for the spiked shoes of bobsledding, she knew she'd be placing herself on a slippery slope. She just never imagined it would be a moral one.

The new Olympic sport of bobsledding—described by sportswriters as a "frozen pool of sharks" and a "two-timing as-the-sled-turns world"—introduced unexpected challenges to the former track star from the University of Alabama at Birmingham. Physically, Flowers had to grapple with the cold. Emotionally, she had to deal with the political climate of the young sport, which was marked by cutthroat partner-switching and backstabbing.

It wasn't easy.

After winning the gold at the Salt Lake Olympics in 2002, Flowers was asked if she would do it again, knowing what she now knew about the sport. She took a moment to contemplate her answer. "I don't know," she replied.

Vonetta Flowers won her first big track race in 1982, at Jonesboro Elementary School. The coach of the Marvel City Striders, DeWitt

Thomas, had come there to recruit the fastest boys and girls for his team. He was surprised to find that a girl recorded the fastest time. Over the next ten years, Flowers won almost every race she entered. Thomas called her "one in a million."

In 1992, Flowers became the first in her family to attend college, accepting a track and field scholarship to UAB, where she competed in the long jump, triple jump and 100-meter dash. At graduation, four years later, Flowers was acknowledged as one of the school's most decorated athletes, racking up thirty-five conference victories in the Penn Relays and the Olympic Festival. She was also the school's first seven-time All-American athlete.

It was a promising start toward her dream of Olympic gold.

Four years later, Flowers qualified for the Olympic trials in Atlanta and Sacramento. She competed in the 100-meter dash and the long jump, but she failed to win a spot on the team.

But Flowers didn't give up. She set her sights on the 2000 Olympic Games—focusing all of her energy into one event: the long jump. Her chances looked good. However, just before the trials, she was forced to undergo ankle surgery. Still on the mend, she competed in the trials, and came in twelfth—not good enough to make the team.

It was enough to convince her to retire from the sport and chase another dream: beginning a family with her husband, Johnny.

But her destiny was waiting in the wings. While at Hughes Stadium in Sacramento, Johnny had picked up a flyer urging track and field athletes to try out for the U.S. bobsled team.

Neither Johnny or Vonetta had ever seen a bobsled—except in the movie *Cool Runnings* about the Jamaican team. They thought about how funny it would be to tell their friends about going to a sled tryout. "For us, it was joke," recalls Flowers. But after several hours of kidding around about it, they made a decision. Johnny, a gifted track and field athlete himself, would give it a shot.

Flowers, still nursing her disappointment from failing to make the Olympic team, agreed to accompany him to nearby UC-Davis for the tryout. After years of competition, she thought she would enjoy finally being in the audience.

Nevertheless, fate took a strange twist: Johnny pulled his hamstring. On a whim, Vonetta stepped in for him and completed the six-part test of speed, strength and jumping ability. She came in second.

It was so crazy that they could hardly believe it. But then Bonny Warner, the woman who had posted the flyer, approached them. Warner told Flowers she might be good enough to win a medal in the 2002 Salt Lake Games, just two years away. Warner herself was a former U.S. luge Olympian-turned-bobsledder.

That was all it took. Almost before Flowers knew it, she was in Germany, learning to push a bobsled. She was amazed by how heavy it was—300 pounds to be exact. When she rode in one a month later, she got another surprise. "No one told me about the g-forces. When I got out, I was dizzy. It was like, 'What have I gotten myself into?' " she recalled.

———————

But Flowers couldn't help but be pleased with her early success. Within two months of the bobsled tryout, she and Warner finished second in the U.S. National Team trials. Now she was traveling to foreign lands competing for the United States as Warner's brakeman.

In the 2000-2001 season, the Warner-Flowers team finished in the top ten in all seven World Cup races. By the end of her rookie season, Flowers and her partner were ranked second in the United States and third in the world. Once again, Flowers began to dream of the Olympics—but this time, a snow-covered one.

Of course, there were problems, too. Flowers was beginning to discover that the word *partner* is used loosely, at best, in bobsledding. Each bobsled team consists of two people: a pilot, whose job is to steer the sled down a track of ice at eighty miles per hour; and a brakeman, whose job is to push the sled hard and fast for the first five seconds of the run, and then jump in and enjoy the ride. Of the two team members, the pilot is definitely in charge. The brakeman is considered expendable.

Coming from the long jump, where Flowers had controlled her own competitive fate, this was a difficult reality to face. "Track, for me, was an individual sport," said Flowers. "I wasn't in a group. I didn't have to depend on anyone."

In bobsled, she soon realized that no matter how well she was doing, her job would always be at risk. So she made herself a promise. First, she would work hard, so she could hold on to her spot. Second, and more importantly, she would not become caught up in the politics of the sport.

Flowers's approach paid off. Her push times (the time it takes to get the sled in motion and get inside the sled) were first-rate—five to six seconds. And she was still improving. She was nearing her one-year anniversary as a brakeman. Everything was going great. And then it happened. Her partner, Warner, the woman who had told her she was good enough to make it to the Olympics, wanted Flowers to have a push-off with brakeman Gea Johnson to see who was better.

Flowers felt betrayed. "I felt I had earned my keep," she said, recalling that her push times had been consistently more impressive than Johnson's. She had worked hard. There was no reason to question her performance. She recalled her promise to herself not to get involved in sport politics—and refused the push-off.

Suddenly Warner cut Flowers from the team.

"She left me," Flowers said. "I went back to Alabama, to my job as assistant track coach at UAB. At that point, that was it for me and bobsled. It wasn't my life. It didn't mean that much. I wanted to start a family."

That was November 2001. A few weeks later, Flowers received an unexpected call. Jill Bakken, a veteran bobsled pilot, invited her to join her team as brakeman. And so, just three months before the Olympics, Flowers was once again racing down the icy track, chasing the illusive dream of a gold medal.

One thing was clear from the first: it was going to be one rocky ride.

Just one week before the Olympic trials, United States bobsled pilot Jean Racine made headlines after she dumped her best friend and brakeman, Jill Davidson, for Gea Johnson. Johnson, in turn, dumped Flowers's old partner Warner.

The media and public cried foul. The timing was unsportsmanlike, leaving Warner and Davidson with too little time to find new partners before the Olympic trials. Unable to find a spot as a brakeman, Davidson eventually had to settle for a position as an Olympic forerunner, which meant she tested the course before the competition. Warner fared better. She scrambled to find a brakeman before the trials. But with little time for practice, Warner and her partner made a poor showing and failed to make the Olympic team.

As a result of the move, Racine gained two titles—one bad, one good. The media dubbed her "Mean Jean Racine." But at the Olympic trials, she and Johnson earned the title of United States 1—the top U.S. women's bobsled team. Bakken and Flowers became United States 2.

Flowers was headed for the Salt Lake City Olympic Winter Games.

In the pre-Olympic hype, two German women's bobsled teams were favored to win gold and silver. The media billed United States 1—the team of Racine-Johnson—as the black horse to medal. Overnight, they became media darlings. Johnson loved it. She posed seminude in *Muscle and Fitness* magazine and appeared on *The Tonight Show* with Jay Leno.

Then, in practice, just days before the Olympics, Johnson's hamstring started giving her trouble. As the competition edged closer, Racine began approaching coaches about replacing Johnson. Two days before the competition, Racine called Flowers to take Johnson's place.

Flowers didn't have to make up her mind. She had made this decision long ago. The conversation lasted just four minutes.

"She asked me if I would leave Jill and compete with her," said Flowers. "I told her no. I was loyal to Jill. I thought we had a chance to win a gold medal."

Bakken said, "I knew Vonetta was loyal. I knew."

February 19, 2002, belonged to Bakken and Flowers from the moment they set foot on the Olympic bobsled track.

In bobsled, winners are determined by the lowest cumulative time of two runs. In the first heat, Bakken-Flowers tied their German competitor's record with a 5.32-second push start time and set a track record of 48.81 seconds. As they crossed the finish line, they instinctively raised their hands in triumph.

Their second run confirmed what they already knew—they had won the gold. "We used to be the other team," Flowers said. "We're *the* team now!"

With a combined run time of just 1:37:76, Flowers became the first black athlete from any country to win a gold medal at a Winter Olympics. Racine-Johnson finished fifth.

On the medal stand at the Utah Olympic Park, Flowers cried as she mouthed the words to the national anthem. In tribute, the German silver and bronze teams lifted Flowers and Bakken onto their shoulders. The United States 2 team was further honored when they carried the flag into the 2002 Olympic Winter Games Closing Ceremonies.

It was a dream come true.

But the story doesn't end there. Just six months after winning a gold medal, Flowers fulfilled yet another dream: she delivered twin boys, Jaden Michael and Jorden Maddox, on August 30, 2002.

You Keep Your Word

"I knew Vonetta was loyal."

These words just speak volumes, don't they? In our minds, they're almost as good as a gold medal.

Bobsled pilot Jill Bakken knew she could trust her brakeman Vonetta Flowers. But how? Because she had seen Flowers keep her word dozens of times before—at practice and in private, in little and big things.

Knute Rockne put it this way: "One man practicing sportsmanship is far better than a hundred teaching it." And when it comes right down to it, there's no other way, really, to establish integrity than to *just do it*. We have to act with integrity over and over, again and again, in every situation, big or small. Through our actions, people learn to trust us. There are no shortcuts.

Now, we've heard people who claim that they can just "sense" a person's level of integrity—that they have some kind of innate character radar. And that may be true, to a point. Joe Badaracco, of Harvard Business School and author of *Defining Moments*, explains it this way: "A lot of our mental processing is unconscious. And the types of human creatures that survived had early warning systems for reliability and trust that we still possess."

But the reality is that trust is usually not granted on a hunch or a feeling. It is earned. It's not something you can fake or rush—or claim for yourself. Like Ralph Waldo Emerson said, "The louder he talked of his honour the faster we counted our spoons."

In other words, we cannot simply talk the talk. Integrity means walking the talk.

"By trust," said Badaracco, "I think you are talking about a kind of reliability, which has to do with 'Will they do what they are committed to do, or duty-bound to do?' Before we put our stamp of approval on someone, we have to see and experience a lot."

When you consider the amount of time required to develop a relationship of trust, you realize something: when someone says they trust us, that's one of the highest compliments we can receive.

"For me, I'd rather be trusted than loved," said Jim Burke, former CEO of Johnson & Johnson, in an interview we conducted with him in 2002. "The more people trust you, the more they think of you. Trust is a synonym for having enormous respect for somebody."

As a ropes-course facilitator, Jay Honey sees people during their most vulnerable moments: on top of a telephone pole, secured by a harness and ropes, held by a coworker.

Businesses from around the United States bring their employees to the ropes course for trust-building seminars. During these activities, employees learn to work together to overcome various physical and mental challenges. The experience culminates on the high ropes course, where employees in harnesses complete physical challenges at a height of thirty-five feet.

"On the high ropes, employees take turns acting as belays for each other," says Jay. "The belay is the person on the ground who keeps your ropes taut and secure when you're on the high course. He is directly tied into your ropes; and it's his job to arrest the fall, if you slip unexpectedly. He's the one who will keep you from getting hurt.

"People are vulnerable on the ropes course. They know that when they climb up the ladder, they are putting all control over their physical well-being into another person's hands. So it's interesting to see which person they choose to put their trust in—and it's usually not the muscleman of the group.

"Physical strength isn't really what matters in this environment. It's the individual with integrity that people want as their belay. They know he'd go to the ends of the earth to keep them safe. They know he's not going to drop them. And when the chips are down, that moral muscle outweighs physical strength every time."

Now, let's return to Bakken's words for just a moment because they beg a most profound question for all of us: what would people expect that you would do in a test of integrity? Would they trust you to keep your word? Would they choose you as their belay?

To quote from our previous book, *The Integrity Advantage:* "To have the Integrity Advantage, you do not lie or cheat on the small things; and, as a result, you are not corrupted by the larger temptations—the lure of power, prestige or money. Just as importantly, if you have integrity, you stick to your internal code of morality, even at the risk of losing your comfortable place in the world."

In the play, *A Man for All Seasons,* the main character, Sir Thomas More (we'll talk more about him later), must choose between losing his head or violating his principles. His reply is pure fiction, but absolutely inspiring, nonetheless:

"When a man takes an oath . . . he's holding his own self in his own hands. Like water. *(He cups his hands)* And if he opens his fingers *then*—he needn't hope to find himself again."

If you're like most people, you need to strive to do better at keeping your word. First, be careful when you make a promise because doing what you say you are going to do is one of the most obvious signs of integrity. Second, start today by setting a goal. A simple, specific one, such as "I will finish all assignments on deadline," is best.

Integrity can be learned. It can be developed. It can be strength-ened. Of course, it takes a little work. But if we're willing to push our-selves, we'll soon find that the results are more than worth the effort. Because whether it's in a bobsled or at the office, people who keep their word usually find themselves leading the pack.

Chapter 6

You Care about the Greater Good

MOTHER TERESA

Integrity Characteristic #6 . . . You Care about the Greater Good

Kindness. Little Agnes Bojaxhiu was born with a magnificent dose of it. As a child, she felt it well up inside her as she prayed and attended daily mass in Skopje, the capital of today's Macedonia. In her adult years, charity and caring poured out of her like cream from a glass pitcher, enveloping the thousands around the world she lifted up, cradled and embraced.

Agnes Bojaxhiu grew to become Mother Teresa, the frail, small-of-stature woman known throughout the world as "The Angel of Mercy," "The Saint of the Gutters" and "The Mother of the Poor." Her decades of serving the poorest among us have redefined the word charity and influenced the lives of millions. Her example of caring for the greater good of all humanity stands as a benchmark that may never be replicated.

But the kindness and love she learned as a child was not purely a reflection of the world around her. Her innate faith, love and caring for others was put to the test even before her tenth birthday.

Agnes's father, Nikola Bojaxhiu, was a member of the municipal council. This gave him power and influence—and one enemy too many. In

1919, following a political gathering in Belgrade, he was killed—apparently poisoned by political adversaries.

The Bojaxhiu children and their newly widowed mother, Drana, now faced the world without a father or husband—a tragedy that can cause even the most devout churchgoers to turn from their guiding principles.

In spite of the desperate situation, Drana remained a devout Catholic. Looking beyond her own suffering, she helped a number of destitute women in her neighborhood. She paid particular attention to one young widow with six children, offering her all of the financial and emotional support she could. When the widow died, leaving her six children parentless, the Bojaxhiu family quickly adopted them into their own fatherless clan.

Agnes's only brother was Lazar, born three years before her. Of his mother's kindness and caring, he said, "She never allowed any of the many poor people who came to our door to leave empty-handed. When we would look at her strangely, she would say, 'Keep in mind that even those who are not our blood relatives, even if they are poor, are still our brothers and sisters.' "

They say an apple never falls far from the tree.

The gentle heart of little Agnes Bojaxhiu grew strong in the shadow of her mother and the church next door, the Sacred Heart of Jesus. At age eighteen, Agnes became an active member of the Daughters of Mary and received what she called an unmistakable and compelling spiritual call to dedicate her life to serving her God. Soon thereafter she boarded a train to Dublin to join the Sisters of Our Lady of Loreto. From there she would travel to Calcutta, her assigned place of service.

"Love is repaid by love alone." She first read these words of Saint Therese of Lisieux on the train to Ireland. They filled her heart and mind—so much so that when she took her vows as a Sister of Loreto, she gave up the name Agnes Bojaxhiu for the name Teresa.

Upon her arrival in India, Sister Teresa was assigned to teach at St. Mary's High School, where she spent seventeen years. Up to this point, she had sacrificed much; but there was more to be done.

In 1946, she became ill with what was suspected to be tuberculosis and was sent to the town of Darjeeling to recover. "It was in the train I heard the call to give up all and follow [Jesus] to the slums to serve him among *the poorest of the poor*," she remembered. Following the call, she asked permission to leave St. Mary's to work outside the convent. Two years later, Pope Pius XII granted her permission. She left the convent with five rupees in her pocket and a $1 sari to live "as an Indian among Indians."

Her first goal was to start a school in the slums of Calcutta for children of the poor. The people of Calcutta, among the poorest in the world, were stunned by her presence among them. Why would this smallish European woman (she was just 5 feet tall) who spoke their language fluently wash their babies, clean their wounds and educate their young? Her compassion astounded them.

It was in the streets of Calcutta where Mother Teresa was approached by one of her former students. The girl asked if she could join Mother Teresa in her lifelong journey of service. Mother Teresa was hesitant; she wanted to make sure this young woman understood the abject poverty she would experience. Several weeks after Mother Teresa asked her to take time to think about it, the girl returned without any personal belongings, wearing a sari, the uniform of the poor. She took her mentor's childhood name as her own and became Mother Agnes. She wouldn't be the last to follow Mother Teresa's powerful example of integrity.

The work was growing. Perhaps the little seed of kindness that had sprouted in the heart of little Agnes of Skopje would blossom into something beautiful.

———————

"Mother" or simply "Ma," as Mother Teresa was widely known, diligently led her order of nuns. They eventually became known as the saving grace of Calcutta. Especially effective during times of natural disaster and war, the presence of the Sisters has remained constant, yet mostly unnoticed. Mother Teresa remarked, "We know what people need, and we start doing it. During floods, the Sisters collect food, while the government provides helicopters to deliver it. Many organizations come forward to help. People give. They help. If everybody does something then the work is done."

Her works are too far-reaching to be bullet-pointed here, but we'll try. In 1952, Mother Teresa established a home for the dying poor— the Nirmal Hriday (or Pure Heart) Home for Dying Destitutes. There, homeless people—uncared for and unacceptable at other institutions— were washed, fed and allowed to die with dignity.

When Pope Paul VI gave her a white Lincoln Continental, she sold the car at an auction and used the money to establish a leper colony in West Bengal.

In 1982, during the siege of Beirut, Lebanon, she persuaded the warring Israeli and Palestinian soldiers to stop shooting long enough for her to rescue thirty-seven children trapped in a frontline hospital.

When the political walls of Eastern Europe collapsed in the late 1980s, she expanded her efforts to communist countries that had previously shunned her, embarking on dozens of new projects.

It was for her tireless labors and endless efforts that she received the Nobel Peace Prize in 1979 for "upholding the sacredness and dignity of every human being . . . [and because] poverty and distress also constitute a threat to peace."

Normally winners of this award are celebrated at a dinner attended by heads of state and honored guests. She refused such a dinner and asked that the money for such an event be donated to the poor. She remarked, "We need to tell the poor that they are somebody to us. That they, too, have been created by the same loving hand of God, to love and be loved."

She accepted the award in the name of the "unwanted, unloved and uncared for," wearing the same $1 white sari she had adopted when she founded her order. Words from her acceptance speech reinforce her legacy of immense caring and compassion:

> *I choose the poverty of our poor people. But I am grateful to receive [the Nobel Peace Prize] in the name of the hungry, the naked, the homeless, of the crippled, of the blind, of the lepers, of all those people who feel unwanted, unloved, uncared for throughout society, people that have become a burden to society and are shunned by everyone.*

Today, what began as one small nun scurrying among the poor in the streets of Calcutta has grown into an order with more than 4,000 Sisters and 400 Brothers running orphanages, AIDS hospices and other charity centers around the world.

Mother Teresa passed away September 5, 1997, at age eighty-seven. Her body was driven through the streets of Calcutta, amongst tens of thousands of mourners, on the same gun carriage that supported Mahatma Gandhi on his last trip through the city. Painted on the windshield was one simple, humble word: *Mother*.

You Care about the Greater Good

A few years ago, when we were just beginning our consulting work, many companies still referred to themselves as "families" and often talked about taking care of each other.

At that time, we were called in to one company, ironically to help with trust issues. What we witnessed was a microcosm of what was happening across North America. During a high-powered meeting, the vice president of human resources informed us that she had banned any words that might imply they were a "family" in all employee communications. "We don't want to imply any responsibility for our employees beyond their legal rights," she said.

To the HR executive, the change was perhaps justifiable from a liability point of view. After all, they *weren't* a family. They had no qualms about firing you if you weren't performing. (On the other hand, when was the last time you laid off your lazy Uncle Vern?)

But the corporate world made this seemingly trivial change without a lot of thought about what the consequences to productivity, commitment and engagement would be. (By the way, as a compromise, we encouraged the company to use the term "community" rather than "family.") Perhaps the omission of that simple, heartfelt word "family" began the long decline in employee-employer relations. Today, too many companies and executives have divorced themselves almost entirely from employees' concerns, goals and lives. Employees have become numbers in these companies; and employees, in turn, see their firms merely as a means to get a paycheck.

Diane Peck, executive director of human resources at Stanford University, explained it this way: "When an employee feels that their boss is either disconnected or hostile, the employee has three options. You either 'go along to get along,' cut your losses and run, or try to change the system. If the problems lie at the top of the system, your chances of changing the system are slim."

From our experience, most employees choose option number 2: cut your losses and run. And the trouble is, we lose the good ones. The ones with options. The ones who stay behind simply tune out. This leads us to what we call a "half employee." As Homer Simpson puts it, "If you don't like your job, you don't quit. You just go in every day and do it half-a**ed. It's the American way."

These "half employees" generate half of the results of engaged employees. They arrive at work not one minute early and leave exactly on time. They perform their work to minimum standards. Many spend a great deal of time looking for a new job: updating their resumes, networking with friends and associates, and searching career Web sites. In other words, they continue to do their jobs, but only at half throttle. What if they could be reenergized?

It can be done—by a leader who is willing to put employees' needs first. You see, even the most stoic among us have emotional needs. In the book *Difficult Conversations*, authors Stone, Patton, Heen and Fischer teach us that our self-worth is dramatically affected by how we answer these three questions:

- Am I competent?
- Am I a good person?
- Am I worthy of love?

When employees answer each in the negative, they, as well as their team, are hurt. If, on the other hand, they answer a resounding "yes!" to each of the questions, they are locked, loaded, primed and polished—ready to be highly productive and efficient.

Which type of employees do you want to show up at work? You decide . . . by the way you treat them.

Just ask James Fitzsimmons of Chicago. His story was highlighted on an episode of the *Oprah Winfrey Show* that studied the ripple effect of kindness. Oprah pulled up to a tollbooth, paid her fare and then paid the toll for a number of the cars to follow.

Fitzsimmons was one of the recipients of this act. After passing through the booth and receiving the $2 gift, he began to think hard about perpetuating this simple act of kindness. At that very moment, he heard on his car radio that nineteen children had been found living in squalor without parental supervision in Chicago. Touched by Oprah's small gift, he wrote a check for $500 for the group of orphans and asked that Oprah's production team make sure the group receive it.

No matter where you are—at the tollbooth or at work—kindness begets kindness.

———

Of all the stories about Mother Teresa, one is particularly moving.

Late one night, a man knocked at the door of Mother Teresa's order and said, "There is a family with eight children. They have not eaten for days."

The good nun took some food to the family. In the faces of the children she did not see sorrow or sadness, just the pain of hunger. She gave the rice to the mother, who divided it, placed half in a container and then walked out the door.

When she returned, Mother Teresa asked, "Where did you go?"

The mother replied, "To my neighbors; they are hungry also."

By caring about the greater good (in other words, caring about our employees' well-being), we break down the walls that separate "us" from "them." In doing so, we avoid costly setbacks created when valuable employees leave.

Chapter 7

You're Honest
but Modest

INTEGRITY WORKS CASE

KATHARINE GRAHAM

Integrity Characteristic #7 . . . You're Honest but Modest

Have you ever had a case of the "woulda-shoulda-couldas"? That's the sick feeling you get when you realize you passed up a gigantic opportunity. Well, here's one of those for you:

It's June of 1971. You've got $10,000 in your checking account and you're looking to invest it. You hear that some young financial advisor named Warren Buffett thinks you should bet on a woman named Katharine Graham, new leader of the Washington Post Company in Washington, D.C. You've never heard of him or her. So you play it safe and plunk your cash into the Dow Industrials.

Twenty years later you sell. Your $10,000 turned into nearly $23,000. "Not bad," you think and reach over your shoulder to pat yourself on the back.

On a whim, you check to see how the Washington Post did. Your jaw drops. You sit down and then look again. Your forehead falls into the palm of your hand. You recheck the numbers. "Could that be?" you ask out loud. You missed out on a $318,000 return. You suddenly have an overwhelming desire to smack yourself silly.

How did a widowed mother of four with no business training turn a struggling newspaper in a male-dominated industry into one of the most successful media companies in the world? We'll tell you, of course, that it was her unique combination of modesty and integrity. Maybe that's painting a complicated and talented leader with too broad a brush. You decide.

———————

Katharine Meyer married "quick-witted, fun-loving" Phil Graham on June 5, 1940. She was a journalist, the daughter of the Washington Post CEO. He was a Harvard Law School graduate, son of a Florida farmer and politician.

On that late spring day, Katharine could not have possibly imagined the daunting challenges and thrilling accomplishments that lay ahead of her. She stepped forward with faith, embarking on a journey that would lead her to the ranks of the world's most influential women . . . and her husband to an early grave.

The mid-'40s were a good time to be young and connected in the capital city. The Grahams socialized with other rising young couples and grew in influence. (After their marriage, John F. and Jackie Kennedy included the Grahams in their circle of friends.) When President Truman asked Katharine's father, Eugene, to head up the World Bank in 1946, he accepted. But not before Phil, his son-in-law, agreed to take his place as publisher of the growing, but still unprofitable, *Washington Post*, which Eugene had purchased in 1933 for $825,000.

The paper continued to grow under Phil's skillful and aggressive leadership, fueled in part by strategic acquisitions of a District of Columbia television station, the *Washington Times-Herald* and *Newsweek* magazine.

They had it all—a growing media business, wealth, connections and their youth. On the surface, the world seemed to be coming up roses for Phil and Katharine Graham.

But roses have thorns.

In October of 1957, buckling under the weight of many responsibilities, Phil suffered an emotional breakdown. Shortly thereafter, he began receiving treatment for mental illness. Despite medical care and the concern of his wife and family, over the next half decade Phil slipped into a downward spiral that included erratic behavior and heavy drinking. On August 3, 1963, shortly after lunching with Katharine at their country house in Virginia, he took his own life. She was the first person to find him.

Katharine had met Phil at a neighborhood party. She fell in love with his "brilliance and charm."

"He was the fizz in our lives," she recalled.

When Phil took over as publisher in 1946, Katharine set aside her reporting career to raise their four children. She was content, she later recalled, to be a dutiful 1950s wife who "liked to be dominated" by the "brilliant, charismatic, fascinating" Phil.

But after his death on that dreadful day in 1963 at Glen Welby farm, everything changed for Katharine and the children. Her choices were to either pull in her sails and succumb to the despair that enveloped her or push forward with determination into the dark fog of unfamiliar waters. She chose the latter.

Though her new life's circumstances were daunting, she was completely determined to keep the paper in the family. In her mind, selling was an unacceptable alternative.

At the beginning of her tenure at the *Post*, she saw herself as little more than a placeholder, making sure the paper stayed within the family. But she quickly rolled up her sleeves and learned the parts of the business she had previously found uninteresting, such as advertising and circulation.

"I did my best to learn, but I made many mistakes," she said. "It was very hard . . . hard on me, hard on people around me." But despite any mistakes she made, Katharine's willingness to work and her dedication to increasing the quality of the *Washington Post* boosted her credibility within the ranks of the editorial and advertising side of the company. The goal, she said, was to put the *Post* among the nation's elite newspapers, and to be "mentioned in the same sentence" as the *New York Times*.

Katharine's first real litmus test came in June of 1971 with the now-famous showdown over the Pentagon Papers, well-chronicled in her memoir, *Personal History*, and in *The Integrity Advantage*. Staring down a number of ideological, financial and legal gun barrels, an anxious but committed Katharine gulped and said, "Let's go. Let's publish." With these words, she galvanized the relationship with her employees.

Former *Washington Post* executive editor Ben Bradlee explained, "The Pentagon Papers experience had forged forever between the Grahams and the newsroom a sense of confidence within the *Post*, a sense of mission and agreement on new goals, and how to attain them."

Katharine and her leadership team faced another stern test one year later when a pair of young reporters named Bob Woodward and Carl Bernstein began a series of stories that linked a burglary at the Democratic Party headquarters to the campaign to reelect President Richard Nixon. The Watergate stories, as they were called, were named for the office complex where the break-in took place. They led to Nixon's resignation in 1974 and a Pulitzer Prize for the *Post*.

From the beginning to the end of the Watergate scandal, Katharine and the *Washington Post* faced intense pressure. Much further ahead in pursuing the scandal than any other news organization, the *Post* felt the ire of President Nixon and his aides. It also came under fire from readers who believed the paper was secretly out to bring down the president.

"It was a particularly lonely moment for us at the paper," Katharine recalled. "I sometimes privately thought: if this is such a great story, then where is everybody else?"

By her own account, however, the most difficult part of her business career was the pressmen union's strike. It began on October 1, 1975, a day after the union's contract was allowed to expire without renewal, and lasted 139 days. Before dawn on the first day of October, an unknown number of pressmen disabled all nine of the presses by ripping out electrical wiring, removing key pieces, jamming cylinders, cutting air hoses and setting fire to part of the pressroom.

Worse even than the vandalism were the personal attacks. At one point during the strike, Katharine noticed a union picketer she had considered a friend carrying a sign saying: "Phil Shot the Wrong Graham."

Katharine's titles and awards are so extensive that we risk boring you by naming them all. But we do it to make a point: this was no ordinary woman.

When Katharine was formally elected president of the Washington Post Company on September 20, 1963, the company owned the newspaper, two TV stations and *Newsweek* magazine. Annual revenues were $86 million. Under her leadership, net income grew from $5 million in 1963 to $175 million in 1991.

On June 15, 1971, eight years into Katharine's tenure as president of the company, Washington Post shares went public at $6.50 per share (adjusted for a subsequent 4-for-1 split). When she stepped down as CEO on May 9, 1991, the price was $222, a gain of 3,315 percent.

Katharine Graham was the first woman to head a Fortune 500 company. Today there are just three. In 1980, she was number one on the *World Almanac*'s list of the twenty-five most influential women. In 1988, *Business Month* magazine named the Washington Post one of the top five best-managed companies in the United States. She has even been inducted into the *Fortune* magazine business hall of fame.

In 1998, Katharine was awarded a Pulitzer Prize for *Personal History*. In her humility, she was stunned.

"I thought I was the peasant walking around among brilliant people."

This statement reflects her modesty. Ben Bradlee once said of her:

"She learned very well and very fast. You know, she learned the way the rest of us learned, by making mistakes and not being scared of saying so."

It was a secret ingredient to her success.

After her career had ended, she admitted to being afraid of asking dumb questions and making mistakes when she first entered the mostly male world of publishing. It's hard to believe, but in preparation for the first company Christmas party following Phil's death, as the new company president she was so anxious about how she would come off that she practiced saying "Merry Christmas" prior to mingling with her guests. She was forty-six years old.

Even later on in her life, when the list of her accolades and triumphs surpassed those of her peers, she doubted her abilities and downplayed her accomplishments—a fact that bonded people to her all the more. At a newsroom celebration of the Pulitzer Prize for her memoir, Katharine expressed honest surprise at winning it. Meg Greenfield, then one of her closest friends and editor of the editorial page, asked her, "Now do you believe you wrote a good book?"

When Allison Pearson of London's *Daily Telegraph* asked Katharine what she might write for her own epitaph, she declined to answer. Allison suggested: "Here Lies Katharine Graham, Who Finally Stopped Apologizing For Herself." Katharine grinned and said, "We'll take that one."

No doubt about it, Katharine Graham was a unique and extraordinary leader. She fought personal demons and doubts with one sword and battled the pressures of being the only female CEO in the country with another. With a third, she took on the trials and dilemmas of running a multimillion- (and later multibillion-) dollar media company. You have to wonder how she did it.

Warren Buffett wrote of Katharine after her passing, "She became responsible for the company's operations in 1963, painfully unsure of herself, but totally sure of her principles. She was never quite sure where debits and credits belonged and couldn't shake the feeling that the lack of an MBA degree destined her for business failure.

"Of course, none of that mattered at all. For Katharine understood the two most basic rules of business: first, surround yourself with talented people and then nourish them with responsibilities and your gratitude; second, consistently deliver a superior, ever-improving product to your customer. Among journalistic leaders, no one carried out either task better than she. The consequence was outsized profits."

Henry Kissinger, former secretary of state, described her as "a symbol of integrity, courage and of high quality."

Even those who suffered under the microscope of *Post* writers seeking the truth understood and respected her value to the American political system. Richard Nixon, who was felled by her reporters, said of her: "In Washington, there are many who read the *Post* and like it and many who read the *Post* and don't like it. But almost everyone reads the *Post*, which is a tribute to Katharine Graham's skill as publisher."

President George W. Bush called her "a true leader and a true lady, steely yet shy, powerful yet humble, known for her integrity and generous to others."

"She was a visionary in the business and media world," said Bill Gates. "She had an extraordinary gift for understanding and connecting with people, and she was a dear friend."

Katharine Graham passed away July 17, 2001, in Boise, Idaho, after suffering head injuries from a fall. She was eight-four years old.

You're Honest but Modest

Individuals with integrity do not proclaim their virtue. They simply lead. Their actions become the purest commentary on their character.

Joe Badaracco, professor at Harvard Business School and author of *Leading Quietly*, says leaders with integrity move quietly "righting—or preventing—moral wrongs in the workplace inconspicuously. . . . Their modesty and restraint are in large measure responsible for their extraordinary achievements."

So it was with Katharine Graham. In an interview for Harvard Business School in 1997, she spoke briefly about her strengths as well as her weaknesses. She said, "I had values and a small sense of organization, but when I started, I really didn't know what an organization was composed of, or whose weight mattered."

By being herself, as vulnerable as that may have made her at times, she gained credibility with her employees. Indeed, she was herself from start to finish. She was genuine. As a result, her associates could trust what she said and did. And that kind of trust creates terrific momentum in an organization.

When she was young, her father, Eugene, once bragged to legendary Washington social figure Alice Roosevelt Longworth, "You watch my little Kate. She'll surprise you."

Sometimes father really does know best.

Chapter 8

You Act Like
You're Being Watched

ABRAHAM LINCOLN

Integrity Characteristic #8 . . . You Act Like You're Being Watched

They didn't call him "Honest Abe" for nothing. Whatever else you may believe about the man who became the sixteenth president of the United States, he always held fast to his principles. In fact, it was sticking to those principles that cost him the U.S. Senate race in 1858.

On June 16 of that year, more than one thousand Republican delegates packed the Springfield, Illinois, statehouse. They named Lincoln the Republican candidate for their seat in the U.S. Senate. He would face off against Stephen A. Douglas, known as the "Little Giant."

At 8 p.m., Lincoln stepped to the podium and delivered his acceptance speech:

> *Mr. President and Gentlemen of the Convention:*
>
> *If we could first know where we are, and wither we are tending, we could then better judge what to do, and how to do it. We are not far into the fifth year since a policy was initiated . . . of putting an end to slavery agitation. Under the operation of that policy, that agitation has not only not ceased, but has constantly augmented. In my opinion, it will not cease until a crisis shall have been reached—and passed. 'A house divided against itself cannot*

stand.' I believe this government cannot endure permanently half slave and half free. I do not expect the Union to be dissolved; I do not expect the house to fall; but I do expect it will cease to be divided. It will become all one thing, or all the other. Either the opponents of slavery will arrest the further spread of it, and place it where the public mind shall rest in the belief that it is in the course of ultimate extinction; or its advocates will push it forward, till it shall become lawful in all the States, old as well as new—North as well as South.

Leonard Swett, a contemporary of Lincoln's, was aghast. He said the speech all but ensured Abe's defeat in the Senate campaign—almost before it began. In his mind, Lincoln had come out with too strong of a statement about slavery.

Lincoln responded simply, "I would rather be defeated with [the 'house divided'] expression in the speech . . . than to be victorious without it." And, as it turned out, he got his way. He lost the Senate race to Douglas, fifty-four votes to forty-six.

But the senate race was just one battle. By the time Douglas was packing his bags for his trip to Washington, Lincoln was well on his way to winning the White House and the war against slavery. His controversial campaign for the Senate had gained him a reputation for speaking his mind. And he had earned his nickname: Honest Abe.

He later explained his philosophy of steadfastly following his convictions: "The probability that we may fall in the struggle ought not to deter us from the support of a cause we believe to be just; it shall not deter me."

In 1860, the hollow-cheeked, lantern-jawed Lincoln was elected president of the United States. He was inaugurated for a second term in 1865.

Shortly after Lincoln won his second term, his former critic Swett admitted he could have been mistaken about the House Divided speech (which is now recognized as one of the most important speeches in American history): "Nothing could have been more unfortunate or inappropriate; it was saying first the wrong thing, yet . . . standing by the speech would ultimately find [Lincoln] in the right place."

For all that has been said about Lincoln, one thing is clear: he always sought to be "in the right place." Both in public and in private.

As a young man, Lincoln, a voracious reader, borrowed the book *The Life of Washington* from Josiah Crawford. At the time, Lincoln lived in a rough-hewn cabin. And just behind the shelf where he stored the borrowed book was a crack in the wall. One night, during a thunderstorm, the rain poured in through the crack and soaked Crawford's book. It was all but ruined.

Lincoln went to Crawford with the news. Together, they determined the book was worth seventy-five cents. And since Lincoln had no money, the two agreed that he would work for Crawford for three days at a rate of twenty-five cents a day to pay for it.

Years later, Lincoln took a job as a store clerk. One day, after tallying up a customer's purchase he felt uneasy. The feeling continued throughout the day. Finally, Lincoln decided to recalculate the transaction. To his consternation, he found he had charged the woman six and a quarter cents too much. To his mind, he had but one choice: to return the money. He knew the woman lived more than two miles away, but that was no matter. That night after closing the store, Lincoln walked to his customer's house and righted the matter.

It wasn't the last time Lincoln's conscience weighed heavily on him. One day, he sold a half-pound of tea. The next morning, as he opened the store, he found a four-ounce weight on the empty scale. He realized that the scale had been improperly balanced when he had measured out the tea the previous evening. The matter bothered him so that he couldn't wait until the end of the business day to make it right. He measured out the four ounces, closed the store and set off to deliver it without delay.

Eventually, Lincoln opened his own store with a partner. But, for whatever reason (and historians list many), it failed within the year. Lincoln was left with his (and much of his partner's) share of the debt. He determined to pay off every cent, although it wouldn't be easy.

To do so, he took two jobs: one as postmaster of New Salem and another as assistant surveyor in northwest Sangamon County. He was often seen tramping through the fields with two or three letters tucked in his hat to be delivered while surveying in the area.

Although his careers changed, Lincoln's commitment to "being morally right" never did. In 1836, Lincoln was licensed to practice law. As an attorney, he was skillful. But his sense of fairness and honesty led him to spend almost as much time persuading people to settle out of court as he did prosecuting cases.

Lincoln said, "Discourage litigation. Persuade your neighbors to compromise whenever you can. Point out to them how the nominal winner is often a real loser—in fees, expenses and waste of time. As a peacemaker the lawyer has a superior opportunity of being a good man. There will still be business enough."

When Lincoln did take issues to court, he most enjoyed a moral victory over a purely financial one. Once he sued a pension agent for charging an elderly widow of a Revolutionary soldier $200 to secure her $400 pension—a 50 percent fee. Lincoln not only offered his services without charge, but he also paid for the woman's hotel room and gave her money for a train ticket home.

Another time, he and a colleague helped save a piece of land owned by a mentally ill girl. According to reports, the case took just fifteen minutes. The real argument occurred when it came time to collect their fee. Lincoln's associate wanted to collect the full amount agreed upon in advance by the girl's brother. Lincoln disagreed: "I am not satisfied," he said. "That money comes out of the pocket of a poor, demented girl; and I would rather starve than swindle her in this manner. You return half the money at least, or I'll not take a cent of it as my share."

Yet another example illuminated Lincoln's character: when a poor man sent Lincoln $25 in payment for his legal services, Lincoln returned $10 of it, saying the payment was overly generous.

Such things happened again and again.

As president, Lincoln continued to hold to his principles. It made him a legend—but also earned him many enemies.

One night, after his election to high office, Lincoln had a nightmare. He was wandering through the White House crying. When he reached the East Room, he came upon an alarming sight: a corpse watched over by an armed guard. "Who is dead in the White House?" he asked the soldier. "The president," answered the soldier.

Five days after Robert E. Lee's surrender to Ulysses S. Grant, effectively ending the Civil War, Lincoln attended a play with his wife at Ford's Theatre. During the performance, he was shot in the back of the head by an assassin. He was carried, unconscious, back to the White House. The next morning, at 7:22, the president was declared dead.

But the memory of his words and deeds—done in private, thought to have gone unnoticed—linger on. They paint a picture of a man who lived like he was being watched—and as it turned out he was.

> *All human beings are endowed with a moral sense. What we do with that sense, how we behave, is up to us. And it is ultimately the sum of our behavior that will dictate our legacy, how we will be remembered.*

—Thomas Jefferson

You Act Like You're Being Watched

One of our friend's daughters keeps a unique china doll on her shelf. It has two faces: one crying, one laughing (one is always hidden by a wig).

Now, that may be fine and good for a doll, but not for us. A person of integrity should not put on different faces for different occasions.

We once heard Michael Josephson, a fantastic speaker, talk about "pet" indiscretions that create questions about our integrity. These are activities that we sense are probably wrong, but we enjoy them so much (or benefit so much from them) that we hate to give them up. It might be as simple as playing Fantasy Football at work. It might be padding the expense account. It might be pushing the envelope when dealing with clients. Whatever it is, it really has its claws into us. So we rationalize. "This won't hurt anything" or "no one has to know about this," we tell ourselves.

"How many times do you get to lie before you become a liar?" asked Josephson. (By the way, no one likes the answer.)

Some try to justify their questionable, on-the-job exploits with such wisdom as, "Work is work; and home is home. And never the twain shall meet."

The problem with this approach is that a lack of integrity—no matter where it occurs or whether anyone sees it—impacts our character. Our lives cannot be compartmentalized. What we do in one aspect of our lives colors all the others.

We discussed the remarkable life of Gandhi earlier in this book. You remember that he spent most of his days pondering and pursuing truth. Not surprisingly, he arrived at the following conclusion:

> *I am firmly of the view, and it is my experience too, that, if a person has violated a moral principle in any one sphere of his life, his action will certainly have an effect in other spheres. In other words, the belief generally held that an immoral man may do no harm in the political sphere is quite wrong. And so is the other belief that a person who violates moral principles in his business may be moral in his private life or in his conduct in family, community or other affairs.*

In other words, we can't keep the ugly face at work and bring the pretty one home. Lincoln understood this well.

On a lighter note, Lincoln was quite homely. In fact, one young girl worried about his appearance enough to write him a letter with some valuable advice. "All the ladies like whiskers," she wrote, "and they would tease their husbands to vote for you and you would be president." Lincoln took this and other comments on his appearance in good humor. He did, however, start growing a beard. When accused of being two-faced, he replied, "I leave it to my audience. If I had two faces, do you think I would wear this one?"

The moral of the story? If you put on your best face in every situation—watched or unwatched—you won't need two.

Bringing our lives into congruence with our principles can be a painful process. But as Axel Munthe, a physician, psychiatrist and writer, said, "A man can stand a lot, as long as he can stand himself." And so it is with the following questions. They may make you uncomfortable for a moment, but they will help you find your "true face" in the long run. We suggest you ask yourself:

- What am I doing that I would be ashamed to have appear in tomorrow's newspaper?
- Is there anything that I feel guilty about, although I'm not really sure it's illegal?
- Is there something I am doing that I would be too embarrassed to describe to my spouse/partner/mother?

If you answer yes to any of these questions, there are areas of your life that have gotten out of sync with your core values. Rather than hide them again, we recommend you make a concerted effort to begin to eliminate them . . . right away.

What you gain in self-respect will more than equal the small, stolen perks you got from the habits you left behind.

Chapter 9

You Hire
Integrity

WARREN BUFFETT

Integrity Characteristic #9 . . . You Hire Integrity

This chapter was the hardest for us to write. The problem was we couldn't agree on whom to write about. We had a number of great options we were mulling over.

Herb Brooks of the *Miracle on Ice* 1980 U.S. Hockey Team certainly put together a collection of players whose character outshined their talent (at least in the beginning of their journey). And the results were extraordinary. We decided to leave him out because we had enough sports figures in the book already.

We then turned to some of the most influential people in history. Some argued that Jesus had put together a group with integrity. Despite their frailties, Peter, Paul, John and the disciples attempted to embody Jesus's prophesy. "Greater works than these shall [you] do," Jesus told his followers. But we had already included religious figures Mother Teresa and Gandhi in the book. And if some considered them to exemplify too high of a standard, how would our readers respond to one who many believe lived a perfect life?

No, we wanted a business leader. So we asked, "Who hires integrity over ability?" The person suggested to us over and over as we bandied this idea among our colleagues was Warren Buffett, chairman of Berkshire Hathaway, Inc.

Sure enough, as we began the research we found we had not even begun to tell Buffett's story.

But we were reluctant to repeat his story. Buffett had played an important part of our first book. And yet, his name kept coming up. So often, in fact, that we finally decided to not ignore the obvious.

Perhaps more than anyone in business today, Warren Buffett hires people based on their integrity. Buffett commented, "Berkshire's collection of managers is unusual in several important ways. As one example, a very high percentage of these men and women are independently wealthy, having made fortunes in the businesses that they run. They work neither because they need the money nor because they are contractually obligated to—we have no contracts at Berkshire. Rather, they work long and hard because they love their businesses.

"And I use the word 'their' advisedly, since these managers are truly in charge—there are no show-and-tell presentations in Omaha, no budgets to be approved by headquarters, no dictums issued about capital expenditures. We simply ask our managers to run their companies as if these are the sole asset of their families and will remain so for the next century."

The unusual thing about Warren Buffett is that he and his longtime partner, Charlie Munger, hire people they trust—and then treat them as they would wish to be treated if their positions were reversed. Buffett says the one reason he has kept working so long (at this point he has scheduled his retirement for five years after his death) is that he loves the opportunity to interact daily with people he likes and, most importantly, trusts.

Consider the following remarkable story from a few years ago at Berkshire Hathaway. It's about R. C. Willey, the dominant home furnishings business in Utah. Berkshire purchased the company from Bill Child and his family in 1995. Child and most of his managers are members of The Church of Jesus Christ of Latter-day Saints, also called Mormons, and for this reason R. C. Willey's stores have never been open on Sunday.

Now, anyone who has worked in retail realizes the seeming folly of this notion: Sunday is the favorite shopping day for many customers— even in Utah. Over the years, though, Child had stuck to his principle— and wasn't ready to rejigger the formula just because Warren Buffett came along. And the formula was working. R. C.'s sales were $250,000 in 1954 when Child took over. By 1999, they had grown to $342 million.

Child's determination to stick to his convictions was what attracted Buffett to him and his management team. This was a group with values and a successful brand.

Arnie Ferrin, longtime friend of Child, said, "I believe that [Child] is a man of extreme integrity, and I believe that Warren Buffett was looking to buy his business because he likes to do business with people like that, that don't have any shadows in their lives, and they're straightforward and deal aboveboard."

This isn't to say Child and Buffett have always agreed on the direction of the furniture store. A few years after the acquisition, Child approached his new boss. He felt that R. C. Willey could operate successfully in markets outside of Utah, even with his closed-on-Sunday policy. Child pitched Las Vegas, but in 1997 they compromised and opened a store in Boise, Idaho.

"I was highly skeptical about taking a no-Sunday policy into a new territory, where we would be up against entrenched rivals open seven days a week," said Buffett. "Nevertheless, this was Bill's business to run. So, despite my reservations, I told him to follow both his business judgment and his religious convictions."

Proving once again that he believed in his convictions, Child insisted on a truly extraordinary proposition: he would personally buy the land and build the store in Boise—for about $11 million as it turned out—and would sell it to Berkshire at his cost if—and only if—the store proved to be successful. On the other hand, if sales fell short of his expectations, Berkshire could exit the business without paying Child a cent. This, of course, would leave him with a huge investment in an empty building.

"I told him that I appreciated his offer but felt that if Berkshire was going to get the upside, it should also take the downside," added Buffett. "Bill said 'nothing doing': if there was to be failure because of his religious beliefs, he wanted to take the blow personally."

You are probably guessing there's a happy ending to the story. And there is. The store opened in August of 1998 and immediately became a huge success, making Berkshire a considerable margin. Today, the store is the largest home furnishings store in Idaho (yes, there *are* other stores in Idaho).

Child, good to his word, turned the property over to Berkshire—including some extra land that had appreciated significantly. And he wanted nothing more than the original cost of his investment. In response, Buffett said, "And get this: Bill refused to take a dime of interest on the capital he had tied up over the two years."

And there's more. Shortly after the Boise opening, Child went back to Buffett, suggesting they try Las Vegas next. This time, Buffett was even more skeptical. How could they do business in a metropolis of that size and remain closed on Sunday, a day that all of their competitors would be exploiting?

But Buffett trusts his managers—because he knows their character. So he gave it a shot. The store was built in Henderson, a mushrooming city adjacent to Las Vegas. The result? This store outsells all others in the R. C. Willey chain, doing a volume of business that far exceeds any competitor in the area. The revenue is twice what Buffett had anticipated.

As this book goes to print, R. C. Willey is preparing to open its third store in the Las Vegas area, as well as stores in Reno, Nevada, and Sacramento, California. Sales have grown to more than $600 million, and the target is $1 billion in coming years.

Buffett, with his tongue firmly in cheek, commented, "Today, when I pontificate about retailing, Berkshire people just say, 'Yeah, but what does Bill think?' I'm going to draw the line, however, if he suggests that we also close on Saturdays.

"You can understand why the opportunity to partner with people like Bill Child causes me to tap dance to work every morning."

Here's another example of Buffett's adeptness at hiring character. He agreed to purchase Ben Bridge Jeweler over the phone, prior to any face-to-face meeting with the management.

Ed Bridge manages this sixty-five-store West Coast retailer with his cousin, Jon. Both are fourth-generation owner-managers of a business started eighty-nine years ago in Seattle. And over the years, the business and the family have enjoyed extraordinary character reputations.

Buffett knows that he must give complete autonomy to his managers. "I told Ed and Jon that they would be in charge, and they knew I could be believed: after all, it's obvious that [I] would be a disaster at actually running a store or selling jewelry (though there are members of [my] family who have earned black belts as purchasers)."

Talk about hiring integrity! Without any provocation from Buffett, the Bridges allocated a substantial portion of the proceeds from their sale to the hundreds of coworkers who had helped the company achieve its success.

Overall, Berkshire has made many such acquisitions—hiring for character first, and talent second—and then asking these CEOs to manage for maximum long-term value, rather than for next quarter's earnings. While they certainly don't ignore the current profitability of their business, Buffett never wants profits to be achieved at the expense of developing ever-greater competitive strengths, including integrity.

It's an approach he learned early in his career.

Warren Edward Buffett was born on August 30, 1930. His father, Howard, was a stockbroker-turned-congressman. The only boy, Warren was the second of three children. He displayed an amazing aptitude for both money and business at a very early age. Acquaintances recount his uncanny ability to calculate columns of numbers off the top of his head—a feat Buffett still amazes business colleagues with today.

At only six years old, Buffett purchased six-packs of Coca-Cola from his grandfather's grocery store for twenty-five cents and resold each of the bottles for a nickel—making a nice five-cent profit. While other children his age were playing hopscotch and jacks, Buffett was already generating cash flow.

Buffett stayed just two years in the undergraduate program at Wharton Business School at the University of Pennsylvania. He left disappointed, complaining that he knew more than his professors. Eventually, he transferred to the University of Nebraska-Lincoln. He managed to graduate in only three years despite working full time.

He approached graduate studies with the same resistance he had approached undergraduate work, but he finally applied to Harvard Business School. In what was undoubtedly one of the worst admission decisions in history, the school rejected him as "too young." Slighted, Warren applied to Columbia where famed investment professor Ben Graham taught.

Professor Graham shaped young Buffett's opinions on investing. And the student influenced his mentor as well. Graham bestowed on Buffett the only A+ he ever awarded in decades of teaching.

While Buffett tried working for Graham for a while, he finally struck out on his own with a revolutionary philosophy: he would research the internal workings of extraordinary companies. He could discover what really made them tick and why they held a competitive edge in their markets. And then he would invest in great companies that were trading at substantially less than their market values.

Ten years after its founding, the Buffett Partnership assets were up more than 1,156 percent [compared with the Dow's 122.9 percent], and Buffett was firmly on his way to becoming an investing legend.

In 2004, Warren Buffett was listed by *Forbes* as the world's second-richest person (right behind Bill Gates), with $42.9 billion in personal wealth. Despite starting with just $300,000 in holdings, Berkshire's holdings now exceed $116 billion. And Buffett and his employees can confidently say they have made thousands of people wealthy.

You Hire Integrity

We often ask business leaders one simple question: which is more dangerous to your firm—the incompetent new hire or the dishonest new hire? It's the part of our presentation where attendees sit up straight and start thinking.

We always follow the question with an exercise on identifying and hiring integrity. Though it becomes obvious that many of the executives and managers haven't given employee integrity much thought, most of the CEOs in the audiences are increasingly concerned about hiring employees with character.

So, how do you hire workers with integrity? It's possible, but not easy. It is important to spend more time choosing a new employee than you do picking out a new coffee machine. Here are a few simple areas to focus on:

First, ensure educational credentials match the resume. Education is the most misrepresented area on a resume. Notre Dame football coach George O'Leary was fired because the master's degree he said he had earned did not exist; the CEO of software giant Lotus exaggerated his education and military service; and the CEO of Bausch & Lomb forfeited a bonus of more than $1 million because he claimed a fictional MBA.

Job candidates also often claim credit for responsibilities that they never had. Here's a typical scenario:

Job candidate: "I led that project. Saved the company $10 million."

Through diligent fact checking, you find an employee at a previous employer who can give you information about the candidate:

Coworker: "Hmm. Actually, Steve was a member of the team, but not the lead. And while it was a great project, we still haven't taken a tally of the cost savings. But ten million seems really high."

How do you find those things out? Confer with companies where the applicant has worked—especially those firms the person isn't listing as a reference. Talk to people inside the organization, going at least two levels deep (which means you ask each reference for a couple more references). Talk to the nonprofit organizations where the person volunteers. Tap into alumni networks and professional associations. Get on the phone with others in the industry to learn about the person's reputation. Check public records for bankruptcy, civil and criminal litigation (with the candidate's knowledge). In other words, check candidates' backgrounds carefully (but legally, of course).

We find that most hiring managers spend 90 percent of their time on capability-related questions, and next to no time on character-based questions. In your rush to get someone in the chair, don't forget to check backgrounds and be rigorous in your interviewing for character. Hiring the wrong person can destroy two careers: your employee's—and your own.

Ask ethics-based questions to get to the character issue. We asked a group of executives at a storage company to brainstorm a list of questions they might ask candidates to learn more about their character. Their list included the following questions:

- Who has had greatest influence on you and why?
- Who is the best CEO you've worked for and why?
- Tell me about your worst boss.
- Who are your role models and why?
- How do you feel about your last manager?
- Tell me about a time you had to explain bad news to your manager.
- What would you do if your best friend did something illegal?
- What would your past manager say about you?
- What does integrity mean to you?

- If you were the CEO of your previous company, what would you change?
- What values did your parents teach you?
- Tell me a few of your faults.
- Why should I trust you?
- How have you dealt with adversity in the past?
- What are your three core values?
- Tell me about a time when you let someone down.
- What is your greatest accomplishment, personal or professional?
- What are your goals and why?
- Tell me about a mistake you made in business and what you learned from it.
- Tell me about a time when you were asked to compromise your integrity.

It's relatively easy to teach a candidate your business. The harder task is trying to instill integrity in someone who doesn't already have it.

Of course, we don't want to imply that it's impossible. Sometimes people will adapt to a positive environment and shine. Some prominent businesses have certainly had tremendous success hiring former prison inmates, demonstrating everyone should have a second chance.

But integrity is a journey that is very personal, very individual. An outside force, such as an employer, typically can't prescribe it. It's certainly not something that happens overnight. That's one reason many of the CEOs we have talked with prefer promoting people from inside their organizations when possible.

Don Graham, chairman and CEO of the Washington Post Company, said, "There's a very good reason for concentrating your hires and promotions on people who already work in your organization. The best way to predict what someone's going to do in the future is to know what they've done in the past—watch how people address difficult business issues, how they deal with the people who work for them, how they deal with the people for whom they work. You may be able to put on a certain face for a day or even a week, but you're not going to be able to hide the person you are for five or ten years."

Graham tells a story about Frank Batten, who for years ran Landmark Communications and founded the Weather Channel. "Frank is a person of total integrity," says Graham. "Frank once said, 'When you go outside for hire you always get a surprise. Sometimes it's a good surprise. But you never hire quite the person you thought you were hiring.' "

What do you usually look for in a job applicant? Years of experience? College degree? Specific skill sets? Or do you look for character? If so, you're in good company.

Years ago, Warren Buffett was asked to help choose the next CEO for Salomon Brothers. "What do you think [Warren] was looking for?" asked Don Graham. "Character and integrity—more than even a particular background. When the reputation of the firm is on the line every day, character counts."

Don't like surprises? Then hire people who have integrity. Want to ensure a good fit with the people you hire? Then hire people who have integrity. Want to ensure your reputation with customers? Then hire people who have integrity.

Are we saying that nothing else matters? No. But we are saying that *nothing matters more*.

Chapter 10

You Stay
the Course

SIR THOMAS MORE

Integrity Characteristic #10 . . . You Stay the Course

Our last story about Sir Thomas More begins not with his birth, but with an impossible dilemma created by a powerful king.

When Arthur, the eldest son of King Henry VII of England, was just three years old, his engagement was announced. He was to be married (in due time) to four-year-old Catherine of Spain, daughter of Ferdinand and Isabella.

As planned, Arthur and Catherine were married twelve years later, in 1501. It was good fortune that in making a good alliance for their countries they also made one for themselves; they immediately fell in love with each other. They lived happily together from October to March of the following year. In March, Arthur fell sick and died—without leaving an heir.

This was a problem for England. It couldn't afford to lose the political alliance with Spain. The only solution that presented itself—marrying off seventeen-year-old Catherine to Arthur's eleven-year-old brother, Henry—was distasteful for more reasons than just their wide difference in ages. The Catholic Church also prohibited a man from marrying his brother's widow: "No man shall marry his brother's widow. It is forbidden.

To do so shames his brother's good name, and the couple shall remain childless" (Leviticus 20:21).

But kings have their resources—and usually their way, too. Soon King Henry's advisors found a Bible verse to counter Leviticus: "If two brothers dwell together and one of them shall die childless, the widow of the dead man must not marry a stranger. Her dead husband's brother shall take her as his wife, and have children by her, and perform all the duties of a husband" (Deuteronomy 25:5).

Delighted, the king immediately ordered the engagement to be arranged, thereby ensuring Catherine's continued presence in England. With that problem resolved, it was not important how soon the marriage itself took place.

In fact, it did not happen before the old king died in April 1509. By then, seven years had passed. Still, to honor his father's wishes, eighteen-year-old Henry went ahead with the marriage to Catherine just a few weeks after his father's burial.

To everyone's surprise, the match appeared to be a good one. Catherine bore many children. Unfortunately, all but one daughter died.

Historians argue about what finally motivated King Henry VIII to seek a divorce from Catherine after more than twenty years of marriage. Certainly, he was under pressure to produce a male heir; and, by then, Catherine was presumed to be barren. Some historians claim that he was bored. Over the years, Catherine is reported to have become increasingly religious (and plain). And there was no doubt that King Henry VIII had fallen in love with a young court attendant named Anne Boleyn. To add to his problems, the public's view of England's alliance with Spain was now unpopular.

For whatever reason, in 1530, one thing was clear: the king wanted a divorce. The problem was, that for all his power, he could not grant it and the pope would not permit it.

In trying to convince the pope of his cause, Henry VIII fell back on the Bible verse in Leviticus. He argued that the Bible forbid such marriages as his. Hadn't all their children died as promised in the scripture?

The pope, possibly experiencing pressure from Spain, argued that the marriage had been consummated, that at least one child had been produced and that it had lasted more than two decades. He would not grant a divorce as long as he was head of the church.

The king found himself in an interesting situation. On one hand, he had always been a strict Catholic—even writing pamphlets to refute Martin Luther's challenges against the church. In return, the pope had bestowed on him the honorable title "Defender of the Faith."

On the other hand, the Defender of the Faith had never before wanted anything to oppose church doctrine or law. Now he did. And that changed everything.

To add to the controversy, it was not long before rumors began to circulate throughout the kingdom that Anne Boleyn was pregnant. Perhaps with a son. Perhaps with the future king! What if he were born illegitimately? Scandalous!

Faced with these pressures, King Henry VIII took matters into his own hands. He embraced the convenient theory that the pope was no more than an ordinary bishop, the bishop of Rome. And if he was simply a bishop, then the pope had no right to appoint other bishops. And if the pope did not, then who did? Didn't he, the king?

Soon a royal proclamation was issued, ordering the clergy to acknowledge Henry as Supreme Head of the Church "as far as the law of God will permit."

———————————

This is the climate in which Sir Thomas More found himself just six months after his first public appearance as Lord Chancellor of England. More, who had once seriously considered the priesthood, had always been a committed Catholic. He also considered himself a loyal subject of the ruler of England.

He now held the highest political and judicial office in England—second only to the king himself. However, his loyalty to the kingdom and the church were at odds. He soon realized he could not compromise his faith: "And there this supple, humorous, unassuming and sophisticated person set like metal, was overtaken by an absolutely primitive rigor, and could no more be budged than a cliff," wrote Robert Bolt in the play *A Man for All Seasons*.

Finding himself unable to support the king's mandate, More immediately submitted his resignation. Because the decision was made so quickly, almost as a reflex, some assumed that it was an easy decision. It was not; for More had much to lose. Bolt wrote, "So far from being one of society's sore teeth he was . . . almost indecently successful. He was respectably, not nobly, born, in the merchant class, the progressive class of the epoch, distinguished himself first as a scholar, then as a lawyer, was made an ambassador, finally Lord Chancellor.

"A visitor's book at his house in Chelsea would have looked like a sixteenth-century Who's Who. . . . He was a friend of the King, who would send for More when his social appetites took a turn in that direction and once walked round the Chelsea garden with his arm round More's neck."

But though More was willing to part with the position of chancellor, the king was not yet willing to part with More. He refused More's resignation.

With no other choice, More dove into his public service, actually exhausting the supply of legal cases in England. His performance was legendary. Even children chanted a popular rhyme about him:

> *When More some times had Chancellor been,*
> *No more suits did remain.*
> *The like will never more be seen,*
> *Till More be there again.*

In the meantime, the Supreme Head of the Church occupied himself with the task of appointing a bishop of Canterbury. The qualifications were clear: the man had to have enough backbone to stand up to Rome, but be willing to submit to Henry's wishes. The king found his man in the form of Thomas Cranmer. In return for his appointment, the new bishop of Canterbury granted Henry a divorce.

During this time, the relationship between More and the king had continued to deteriorate. In many conversations with King Henry, More had explained his objections to the ruler's divorce and assumption of papal power to no avail. Finally, in May 1532, the king accepted More's resignation. More had held the position of chancellor for fewer than three years.

For More, this meant the loss of all income except for a modest rent from some property. He happily reduced his lifestyle. For almost two years, he lived in seclusion, spending much of his time writing. He did not attend Anne Boleyn's coronation.

Then, in March 1534, the Act of Succession was passed. It required all who were called upon to take an oath acknowledging Henry and Anne as legitimate heirs to the throne. On April 14, More refused to take the oath. He was committed to the custody of the abbot of Westminster. Four days later, he was removed to the Tower of London prison.

While there, he suffered from "his old disease of the chest . . . gravel, stone and the cramp." But you would not have known it for his merry countenance when friends and family visited. He continued to write, which had always been one of his passions. During his time in prison, he completed several treatises. As strange as it may seem, for all appearances, More remained very much unchanged by the tumult around him.

In *The Life of Thomas More*, William Roper explained it this way:

> *Thus being so well and quietly settled in conscience, the security and uprightness of the same so eased and diminished all the griefs and pains of his imprisonment and all his other adversity, that no token or signification of lamenting or sorrow appeared in*

him, but that in his communication with his daughter, with the Lieutenant and others, he held on his old merry, pleasant talk.

Bolt explained More's reaction in the same way:

[More] was a person who could not be accused of any incapacity for life, who indeed seized life in great variety and almost greedy quantities, who nevertheless found something in himself without which life was valueless and when that was denied him was able to grasp his death.

In April and May of 1535, More was asked his opinion of the new statutes conferring on Henry the title of Supreme Head of the Church. More declared only that he was a faithful subject of the king.

When it later was discovered that More had written to the bishop of Rochester while in prison, More's books and writing utensils were taken away. Still, he wrote as much as he could to his wife and daughter, using stray scraps of paper and charred sticks or pieces of coal.

Then, on July 1, More was convicted of high treason for denying the power of parliament to confer ecclesiastical supremacy on King Henry VIII.

More was beheaded on the Tower Hill on the morning of July 6.

Shortly before his death, More wrote to his daughter. "My case was such in this matter, through the clearness of my own conscience, that though I might have pain, I could not have harm; for a man may, in such a case, lose his head and not have harm."

There is some evidence, for the religiously minded, that he was right. In 1935, 400 years after More's death, he was canonized by Pope Pius XI.

He held his course, and for this reason, above all others, we hold tightly to his memory.

You Hold the Course

Not your typical happy ending, right? Well, there's more.

After his death, More's head was parboiled and displayed on

London Bridge for a month. Afterwards, his daughter retrieved it from the man who was supposed to throw it into the river. In 1824, a lead box was found in the Roper family vault. When opened, it was found to contain a head, assumed to be More's.

Fortunately for us, More left behind much more. He gave us a legendary model of a life of integrity, a life in striking contrast to that of his king.

Although the two of them met at the same moral crossroads, they took different paths. One changed like a chameleon to match the changing scenery—and his changing desires. The other held his course. It reminds us of the last few lines of the famous poem by Robert Frost *The Road Not Taken:*

> *Two roads diverged in a wood, and I—*
> *I took the one less traveled by,*
> *And that has made all the difference.*

Consider, for a moment, the difference in how the world remembers King Henry VIII and Sir (or Saint) Thomas More. Henry is characterized solely by his appetites. Typical of most historians, Robert Bolt describes him this way: "Henry VIII, who started with everything and squandered it all, who had the physical and mental fortitude to endure a lifetime of gratified greeds, the monstrous baby whom none dared gainsay."

In contrast, More is immortalized as a man of unwavering character: "More is a man of an angel's wit and singular learning," wrote Robert Whittinton. "I know not his fellow. For where is the man of that gentleness, lowliness and affability? And as time requireth a man of marvelous mirth and pastimes; and sometimes of a sad gravity: a man for all seasons."

Samuel Johnson put it simply: "He was the person of the greatest virtue these islands ever produced."

These words paint a vivid picture, don't they? A monstrous baby and a man of an angel's wit. One with integrity. One without.

The difference between the two was their ability (or inability) to hold the course, regardless of outside pressures. Both had much to lose in the moral crisis they faced. One was willing to sacrifice his integrity. The other was willing to lose everything but his honor.

Life's constant distractions make staying the course difficult. Society will always be tugging at our sleeves, offering different courses, tempting us to "broaden our horizons."

But beware. There is an old saying we've heard more than once, but unfortunately can't attribute: "Some people say they are broadminded, when it's only their consciences stretching." If you look around you, it's clear that today, most people are morally stretched beyond limit. So much so, that a person with integrity is a rare find.

It's ironic, really. When we see how hard some of us try to set ourselves apart—by achievement, lifestyles, cars, houses, clothes, hairstyles (and even body piercings)—we realize that the people who are truly unique are those with integrity.

And here arises another difficulty. It is impossible to hold the course if you're a follower. That's because society (and most of the people in it) are in constant moral flux. Their values are fluid.

"Society can have only as much idea as we have about what we are about, for it has only our brains to think with," said Robert Bolt in the preface to *A Man for All Seasons*. "And the individual who tries to plot his position by reference to our society finds no fixed points, but only the vaunted absence of them."

We've heard it said that "a man in step with society . . . is out of step with himself." And it's true. Thomas More understood this.

In his *Dialogue on Conscience*, which he wrote in prison, More stated, "I never intend, God being my good Lord, to pin my soul on another man's back, not even the best man that I know, this day living; for I know not where he may hap to carry it."

A person of integrity takes responsibilities for her own decisions. And, as such, she chooses her own consequences, and directs her own fate.

In dialogue from *A Man for All Seasons*, the Duke of Norfolk attempts to persuade Sir Thomas More to swear an oath supporting the Act of Succession:

> NORFOLK: *Oh, confound all this . . . I'm not a scholar, as Master Cromwell never tires of pointing out, and frankly I don't know whether the marriage was lawful or not. But damn it, Thomas, look at those names. . . . You know those men! Can't you do what I did, and come with us, for fellowship?*
>
> MORE: *And when we die and you are sent to heaven for doing your conscience, and I am sent to hell for not doing mine, will you come with me, for fellowship?*

This is a fictional dialogue, but with it Bolt makes an important point: in the end, we alone are responsible for our choices, good or bad. And we alone must face the consequences of those choices. That's why it's so important that we establish our own set of guiding principles and follow them unerringly.

We've thought of this point often while flying over the Midwest. Looking down on hundreds of thousands of acres of planted fields, we have marveled at the uniformity of the rows. How is it done? We've been told that a farmer fixes his sight on a landmark at the opposite end of the field and guides his plow toward it. By keeping his eye on the landmark, he keeps his furrow straight.

The same principle can work for us, too. We must set our moral course, and then fix our sights firmly on it. There will be many distractions along the way, but we can't let ourselves be led awry by what happens around us. We must first determine and then hold our course at all costs.

And, at the end of it all, we will discover we have grown into something rare and extremely valuable: a person of integrity.

"Lives of great [people]
all remind us we can make our lives sublime,
and departing, leave behind us
footprints on the sands of time."
— Henry Wadsworth Longfellow

INTEGRITY AT WORK

What story will our footprints tell to those who come after us? More importantly, what path will it lead them on should they choose to follow?

Our lives don't play out in a vacuum. Like it or not, our individual choices inevitably impact those around us: Our employees. Our company. Our community. Our children. It is imperative then to live with integrity. As Will Rogers liked to quip, "Live in such a way that you will not be ashamed to sell your parrot to the town gossip."

In fact, stories of lives filled with integrity simply beg to be retold. Here's one we like to retell occasionally:

A few years ago, a neighbor's son was a football player on the high school team. On away games, the athletes would get together after hours, many of them to sneak out, drink, or . . . well, you've probably known a few teenage boys in your day (or have been one). But Jake wanted no part of the shenanigans. Jake not only said no, but also let the other guys know what he thought they should be doing instead as representatives of their school.

It's important to note that Jake wasn't the best player on the team. He was a slow, 180-pound defensive lineman. But maybe that's why the others started to pay attention to him. He was one of them. Pretty soon, when faced with a moral choice, even the coaches started asking, "What would Jake do?"

A small moral victory, sure. A blip on the integrity Richter scale, maybe. But for the coaches, players and families of that football team, it taught a clear lesson that they all understood—and embraced. One footprint in the sand.

Now, imagine the impact when many people of integrity unite within one company. What could be achieved? Well, that's just what CACI, a 9,400-employee technology company headquartered near Washington, D.C., is trying to accomplish.

Jack London, their chairman, president and CEO, affirmed, "Our deep commitment to business integrity guides employees' behaviors when specific direction is lacking. For example, when an employee faces a quandary, he instinctively applies our established business values without having to turn to a methods and procedures handbook. This ensures that we are always ready to respond to client needs, because we know the rules, the boundaries and our goals—by heart."

CACI is wise to employ this philosophy. In fact, a recent study showed that companies with a strong ethics program ranked an average of fifty places higher on the *Business Week* 500 List.

Recently, CACI employee Dennis Kennedy received recognition from the firm for the integrity he displayed while doing work for a large military client. The job was to install a Readiness Management System (used to determine the status of armed forces units worldwide).

"The client thought it would take four to five days to install and get a Java Web application running," Kennedy said. "But we had the Web application, server application and first users running in just a few hours. They were very pleased." In some organizations, employees or their leaders might have been tempted to fudge the numbers and pad the bill. After all, wasn't this big bureaucratic military organization expecting to pay for a few days of work, not a few hours? Who would ever know? The people at CACI, that's who.

Because employees do their jobs with integrity and high standards, CACI customers know the products and services will be first-rate. As a result, the financial results from these types of integrity-based business practices have been outstanding. CACI is growing by leaps and bounds as customers come to know they can trust the company, and investors remain confident that their money will bring a better-than-average return.

At CACI, and other companies like it, integrity has a domino effect. It builds and inspires employee leadership, which motivates employees to perform at higher levels, which, in turn, inspires customer and shareholder loyalty.

It is critical that integrity resides in employee minds and hearts (rather than being tucked away in some employee handbook). If you stuff ethics in a handbook somewhere and never air them in the office, the effects of integrity will stop cold. Employees' integrity should be evident in their actions, and the truth should always be on the tips of their tongues. Most importantly, their commitment to honesty should go straight to their hearts.

And once that happens, you can be sure your company is on the path to success.

Difficult Decisions

Of course, when we put integrity into action, we are subject to the laws of motion: for every action, there is an equal and opposite reaction.

Ed Nusbaum, CEO of Grant Thornton, LLP, worries a lot about this dilemma. His industry—tax and accounting—has been rocked by scandal over the past few years. And, while Grant Thornton has a sterling reputation for integrity, Nusbaum realizes the land mines inherent in the industry could bring his organization to its knees if its leaders are not very careful.

Nusbaum told us, "When we live with integrity, we will inevitably be faced with difficult decisions. In nearly every aspect of our business, we confront gray areas. Even though we are experts, when analyzing accounting pronouncements and tax regulations, there is not always one right answer. In these critical situations, we must apply the spirit of the law, rather than letter of the law, requiring us to exercise judgment. A sound level of integrity will help us and our clients make appropriate decisions."

Recently, Grant Thornton was presented with an opportunity to accept a new, highly lucrative client. However, the senior partners were not entirely comfortable with the company's financial prospects and, more importantly, the integrity of the company's management. Nusbaum said, "We decided to decline the opportunity. As it turns out, one of our competitors accepted the work and just a few months later fraud was uncovered. The company is now in bankruptcy."

Nusbaum continued, "The integrity of our team saved the firm from potential legal issues and unfavorable publicity. In short, it preserved the reputation that all of us work so hard to uphold—every day, on every engagement."

So often in business, you push forward with your goals; but reality pushes back. The choices you make at those times are what separate great leaders from average or poor leaders. Leaders like Nusbaum, who strive to lead by and with strong principles, realize that they are the teachers of integrity in their organizations. They know that even small decisions made in private can shape the character of their companies, and their actions and omissions send signals to their constituents. This knowledge gives them the power to hold their moral ground when push comes to shove.

As a leader, you face these difficult decisions every day. Soon after the release of our first book, we spoke to members of the Young Presidents Organization. Several of these high-powered executives cornered us after the speech and spoke passionately about their real-life integrity challenges.

"It'll be the ethical decisions that eventually drive me to sell my company," said one man, still in his thirties. We hope he stays in business because it's his concern about integrity that makes him a great leader, a leader his employees follow willingly.

While we don't have the answers for every difficult question you will face, we do believe we have a way to help you make decisions that you can look back on with a sense of accomplishment, honor and pride. Try answering these simple questions when you are forced to make decisions about gray areas of business:

- What does my intuition tell me?
- What have I promised?
- Which value do I care most about?
- Have I sought counsel from people with integrity?
- Will this decision move me toward goals I care about?

Using this very simple model, it is possible to make better decisions that will increase the luster of you and your organization—both externally and internally. Never forget that a reputation is attached to us wherever we go in life. It is our personal brand, and in many ways measures how much we are trusted and respected.

As we close, we would like to share a thought-provoking poem with you. Often, people get quite worked up when we say it is anonymous, claiming that so and so wrote it. However, after extensive research, we have found it is attributed to many different people. So while we would love to give credit where it is due, we just can't say with surety who wrote it.

Be careful of your thoughts,
for your thoughts become your words.
Be careful of your words,
for your words become your deeds.
Be careful of your deeds,
for your deeds become your habits.
Be careful of your habits,
for your habits become your character.
Be careful of your character,
for your character becomes your destiny.

In parting, we caution you to be careful out there. Our destinies don't happen, as many people suppose. We create them through our daily actions and habits. As you carefully apply the principles illustrated within these chapters, integrity will shape your character. And when it does, magical things happen.

Remember that inspiring quote from George MacDonald from earlier in the book? He said, "Few delights can equal the mere presence of one we trust utterly."

Do you wonder what it would be like to have people trust you utterly? To delight in your presence? To willingly follow you and respect you? By implementing the characteristics of integrity in your work and your life, we believe you'll soon find out.

Sources

BOOKS

Adams, Simon. *Mahatma Gandhi: The Father of Modern India*. New York: Raintree Steck-Vaughn Publishers, 2002.

Alger, Horatio. *Abraham Lincoln, The Backwoods Boy; or How a Young Rail Splitter Became President*. New York: Polyglot Press, 2002.

Ash, Mary Kay. *Mary Kay on People Management*. New York: Warner Books, 1984.

Ash, Mary Kay. *Mary Kay: The Story of America's Most Dynamic Businesswoman*. New York: Perennial Currents, 1994.

Badaracco, Joseph L., Jr. *Defining Moments. When Managers Must Choose Between Right and Wrong*. Cambridge: Harvard Business School Press, 1997.

Basler, Roy P. *Lincoln: His Speeches and Writings*. Cleveland, OH: Da Capo Press, 2001.

———. *The Collected Works of Abraham Lincoln/First Supplement 1832–1865*. Reissue ed. Piscataway, NJ: Rutgers UP, 1990.

Bolt, Robert. *A Man for All Seasons*. Vintage International ed. New York: Vintage, 1990.

Botkin, B.A. *A Treasury of American Folklore*. New York: Crown Publishers, 1944.

Bush, Catherine. *Gandhi (World Leaders Past and Present)*. New York: Chelsea House Publications, 1985.

Cherrington, Jay Owen, and David Jack Cherrington. *Moral Leadership and Ethical Decision Making*. Provo, UT: CHC Forecast, Inc., 2000.

Gandhi, Mahatma, and Raghavan Iyer. *The Essential Writings of Mahatma Gandhi*. Oxford: Oxford UP, 1990.

Gandhi, Mohandas K. *An Autobiography: The Story of My Experiments with Truth*. Reprint ed. Boston: Beacon Press, 1993.

Gostick, Adrian, and Dana Telford. *The Integrity Advantage: How Taking the High Road Creates a Competitive Advantage in Business*. Layton, UT: Gibbs Smith, Publisher, 2003.

Graham, Katharine. *Personal History*. New York: Random House, 1997.

Keneally, Thomas. *Abraham Lincoln*. New York: Viking Penguin, 2003.

Khan, Adam. *Self-Help Stuff That Works*. Bellevue, WA: YouMe Works, 1999.

Kouzes, James, and Barry Posner. *Credibility: How Leaders Gain and Lose It, Why People Demand It.* San Francisco: Jossey-Bass, 2003.

Martin, Christopher. *Mohandas Gandhi.* Minneapolis: Lerner Publications Company, 2001.

More, Thomas. *Four Last Things: The Supplication of Souls: A Dialogue on Conscience.* New York: Scepter Publishers, 2002.

Mother Teresa. *A Simple Path.* New York: Ballantine Books, 1995.

———. *In the Heart of the World: Thoughts, Stories, & Prayers.* Ed. Becky Beneate. Novato, CA: New World Library, 1997.

———. *My Life for the Poor.* Eds. Jose Luis Gonzalez-Balado and Janet Playfoot. New York: Ballantine Books, 1985.

———. *No Greater Love.* Novato, CA: New World Library, 1997.

Roper, William. *Life of Sir Thomas More.* Springfield, IL: Templegate Publishers, 1978.

Schlossberg, Dan, and Jay Johnstone. *The Baseball Almanac.* South Bend, IN: Triumph Books, 2002.

Steelcase, Inc. *Office Environment Index Summary Report.* Grand Rapids, MI: Steelcase, Inc.,1991.

Stone, Douglas, Bruce Patton, and Sheila Heen. *Difficult Conversations: How to Discuss What Matters Most.* New York: Penguin Books, 1999.

Wooden, John, and Jack Tobin. *They Call Me Coach.* Lincolnwood, IL: Contemporary Books, 1997.

Wooden, John, and Steve Jamison. *Wooden: A Lifetime of Observations and Reflections On and Off the Court.* Lincolnwood, IL: Contemporary Books, 1988.

FILM

Kempner, Aviva. *The Life and Times of Hank Greenberg.* VHS and DVD. Directed by Aviva Kempner. Los Angeles: Twentieth Century Fox, 1998.

LECTURES

The Graham Family and the Washington Post Company. Harvard Business School Case 9 – 498-031. 1997.

Lear, Norman. "Social Responsibility: A Cure for the Loneliness in Our Time." Harvard Divinity School and Harvard Business School, Cambridge, 1998.

PERIODICALS

Olmsted, Larry. "The Good, the Bad, and How to Tell the Difference." *American Way Magazine*, November 2003.

Reilly, Rick. "A Paragon Rising above the Madness." *Sports Illustrated*, March 20, 2000.

Smith, J. Y., and Noel Epstein. "Katharine Graham Dies at 84: She Guided Post through Pentagon Papers and Watergate to Fortune 500." *Washington Post*, July 18, 2001.

Willing, Richard. "Washington Post Icon Katharine Graham, 84, Dies." *USA Today*, July 18, 2001.

ONLINE SOURCES

"Abraham Lincoln." Terraformers Tombtown: Virtual Home of the Living Impaired. http://www.tombtown.com.

"Abraham Lincoln Quotes." BrainyMedia.com. http://www.brainyquote.com.

Associated Press. "Mary Kay Cosmetics Founder Dies at Age 83." USAToday.com. http://www.usatoday.com/news/nation/2001/11/22/marykay-obit.htm.

"The Awards for Alumni Achievement." Harvard Business School. http://www.alumni.hbs.edu/alumni_achievement/burke.html.

Basler, Roy P., ed. "Abraham Lincoln Online: Speeches and Writings." Abraham Lincoln Online. http://www.showcase.netins.net/web/creative/lincoln/speeches/house.htm.

Bindra, Satinder. "Needing a Miracle, She Found One." CNN.com. http://archives.cnn.com/2002/WORLD/asiapcf/south/10/01/mother.teresa.saint/index.html.

Broderick, Robert C. "The Catholic Encyclopedia." Robert Appleton Company. http://www.newadvent.org.

Flowers, Vonetta. "Vonetta Flowers." Vonetta Flowers. http://www.vonettaflowers.com.

"Hall of Famers." Naismith Memorial Basketball Hall of Fame. http://www.hoophall.com/halloffamers/Wooden.htm.

"The Hall of Sports: John Wooden." Academy of Achievement: A Museum of Living History. http://www.achievement.org/autodoc/page/woo0int-1.

"Hank Greenberg." Jewish-American Hall of Fame.
http://www.amuseum.org/jahf/virtour/page26.html.

"Hank Greenberg." Jewish Virtual Library.
http://www.jewishvirtuallibrary.org/jsource/biography/greenberg.html.

"Hank Greenberg." National Baseball Hall of Fame.
http://www.baseballhalloffame.org/hofers_and_honorees/hofer_bios/green-berg_hank.htm.

"Highlights of Mother Teresa's Life." CNN.
http://www.cnn.com/WORLD/9709/mother.teresa/chronology/index.html.

"John Wooden: Like UCLA, Simply the Best." Billwalton.com.
http://www.billwalton.com/wooden.html.

Jonas, Donald K. "The New Golden Rule." March 28, 2000. Hudson Institute.
http://www.hudson.org.

Kahn, Adam. "Honest Abe." Healthy Place, Inc.
http://www.thisisawar.com/InspirationAbe.htm.

"Katharine Graham Dies." PBS, July 17, 2001.
http://www.pbs.org/newshour/media/media_watch/jul-dec01/graham_7-17.html.

"Legendary Washington Post Chief Kay Graham Dies." CNN.
http://www.cnn.com/2001/ALLPOLITICS/07/17/obit.graham.

"Legendary Washington Post Chief Kay Graham Dies." CNN.
http://www.cnn.com/2001/ALLPOLITICS/07/17/obit.graham/index.html.

"Mary Kay Ash." FamousTexans.com.
http://www.famoustexans.com/MaryKayAsh.htm.

Marzejka, Laurie J. "The Tigers' 'Hammerin' Hank' Greenberg." The Detroit News.
http://info.detnews.com/history/story/index.cfm?id=129&category=sports.

"Mother Teresa." Lifetimetv.com.
http://www.lifetimetv.com/shows/ip/portraits/9629/9629_bio.html.

"Mother Teresa: The Early Years." EWTN Global Catholic Network.
http://www.ewtn.com/motherteresa/index.htm.

"Mother Teresa: The Passing of a Saint." Ability Magazine.
http://www.abilitymagazine.com/teresa_story.html.

"Mother Teresa: A Profile." CNN.
http://www.cnn.com/WORLD/9709/mother.teresa/profile/index.html.

Norton, R. J. "A Brief Biography of Abraham Lincoln." Abraham Lincoln Research Site. http://members.aol.com/RVSNorton1/Lincoln48.html.

"The Pyramid of Success." http://www.coachwooden.com.

"Saint of the Gutters." CNN. http://www.cnn.com/WORLD/9709/mother.teresa/impact/index.html.

Schudson, Michael. "Watergate: A Study in Mythology." Columbia Journalism Review, May/June 1992. http://archives.cjr.org/year/92/3/watergate.asp.

Singer, Andrew W. "The Perils of Doing the Right Thing." The Conference Board. http://www.conference-board.org/articles/atb_article.cfm?id=153.

Smith, J. Y., and Noel Epstein. "Katharine Graham Dies at 84." Washington Post, July 18, 2001. http://www.washpost.com/history-kgraham-obituary.htm.

Sneller, Rhoda, M.S.J., and Lowell Sneller, Ph.D. "House Divided Speech." Abraham Lincoln Online. http://www.showcase.netins.net/web/creative/lincoln/speeches/house.htm.

"Texas Women's Hall of Fame: Mary Kay Ash." Texas Women's University. http://www.twu.edu/twhf/tw-ash.htm.

"Tributes." Mary Kay: Departed this Life November 22, 2001. http://www.marykaytribute.com/Tributes2.htm.

"Washington Post Head Katharine Graham Dies." Local6.com. http://www.local6.com/news/876364/detail.html.

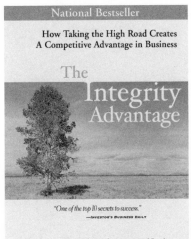

Also by Dana Telford and Adrian Gostick
The Integrity Advantage
A NATIONAL BESTSELLER
ISBN 1-58685-246-9, $18.95 hardcover

Available wherever books are sold, or from

www.gibbs-smith.com

"This is the best business book I've read in at least a year!"
—Chester Elton, coauthor, *The 24-Carrot Manager*

"*The Integrity Advantage* is, by definition, essential to success
as a leader. . . ." —Dr. Lynn Newman, MBA faculty,
Pepperdine University

"This book is a must-read for everyone, but most importantly
for businesspeople who believe the only measure of the company's value is in its financial statement." —Mike S. West,
vice chairman, Rayne Corporation